Affordable Homes

for every stage of life

D1300774

Pr____ ____ 00 easy-living home plans from Donald A. Gardner Architects, Inc.

Timelines are not measured by years, but by milestones, transitions, turning points and passages. It seems these markers usher in the many chapters of an individual's life. Much like words on a page, each chapter is filled with memories that define that time.

Aside from pictures and home-movies, many memories are stored within the mind. However, the remnants that commemorate those special times might be lying about the house. The first dollar your business ever made could be framed and hanging in your home office. Your seasonal decorations might be tucked away in the attic, waiting for the holidays.

Proven again and again, it takes family and friends to turn a house into a home. It's the living that makes the transition unique. It's the slamming of the front door and high-pitched squeal that alerts the family of an earned A+ on a tough exam, or a middle-of-the-afternoon phone call that details a well-deserved vacation.

So in elevating the quality of life, it's only fitting that homes not only be functional and affordable but conducive to living. Within these pages you'll discover a collection of homes designed for every stage of life. From the milestones and transitions to the turning points and passages, these homes encourage each chapter of your life, housing your memories and remnants, making even the day-to-day a little more special.

A DESIGNS DIRECT PUBLISHING BOOK

Presented by

DONALD A. GARDNER
ARCHITECTS, INC.

Donald A. Gardner Publishing, LLC
Angela Santerini, President
Dominic Foley, Publisher
Kathleen Nalley, Editor
Paula Powers, Writer
Jenni McLaughlin, Graphic Artist

Donald A. Gardner Architects, Inc.
Donald A. Gardner, CEO
Angela Santerini, President

Illustrator Credits
Architectural Art
Greg Havens
Barry Nathan

Photographer Credits
Matthew Scott Photographer, Inc.
Riley & Riley Photography, Inc.
Stephen Stinson Photography
Windward Photography

Cover photo by Matthew Scott Photographer, Inc., Charleston, SC
Printed by Toppan Printing Co., Hong Kong

First Printing: August 2004

10 9 8 7 6 5 4 3 2 1

Table of Contents

What makes a home affordable?

Home affordability is a broad subject with many factors to determine it. What constitutes affordability for one person may not be the same for another, and construction costs vary depending on location. Realizing there are so many deciding factors that comprise affordability, you don't have to know them all right away, but you should at least focus on the essential ten. Before choosing a house plan, you'll want to consider budget, financing, location, lot, permits/fees, land-use regulation, house specifications, materials, labor and utilities.

Budget

Even though your budget is the most obvious factor, it is still worth mentioning, because it is one of the most important. A good rule of thumb is to choose a home that costs no more than four times your salary to purchase. Base your figure on what you are currently making, not on potential raises or bonuses, because a cost of living increase may invalidate the additional monies.

Financing

According to the Federal Housing Administration, no more than 29 percent of your gross monthly income should be allotted for your mortgage payments. You'll need to think about interest rates and any other items such as insurance and property taxes that you might like to include within your monthly payment. Keep in mind that this figure may differ when you consider your debt-to-income ratio.

Location

You've heard it's all about location, but it's truer than you might realize. You'll pay more for a beautiful coastal lot with a prime view, because coastal homes must meet more stringent building codes. In order to meet local conditions, additional reinforcements may be necessary, increasing construction costs.

Lot

Going hand-in-hand with location is the lot itself. Besides the actual dimensions and outline of the lot, the surface and elevation are important. A challenging lot such as a sloped or mountainside lot will incur more expenses if blasting, grading or preparations for equipment/material access is needed.

Taking a progressive approach to home affordability, you may even want to have a few tests performed on your lot to curtail any future problems. Some tests may be free; others will involve charges. You may decide that you only want one or two, so here are the most common: a survey defines the property; a site analysis reports soil types and conditions; a topographical reading details elevation changes; and a floodplain request indicates if any portion of your lot is in danger of flooding. Wind, solar and temperature patterns of your area, and specifically your lot, can be obtained from local agencies.

Permits/Fees

Aside from your building permit, you may acquire a few fees. Depending upon where you're building, you may be required to pay fees to an Architectural Review Committee or Board, and you might have to pay property owners' association dues. If you're building in the country, find out if the road to your property is a public or private road; you may have to buy access or obtain a legal easement.

8

Affordable Homes • The Designs of Donald A. Gardner Architects, Inc.

Land-Use Regulation

Zoning is probably the biggest element under land-use regulation. Knowing local zoning laws assists you in understanding what you can and can't do with your land, which helps you avoid future problems. You may be allowed to have livestock on your property. You may not be able to operate a business from your house. You may or may not be allowed to build an additional out-building; if you are allowed to have an out-building, it might increase your property taxes.

Contingent on where you build, you may have to meet covenants — those rules and regulations set forth by a governing body. Satisfying covenants might require additional expenses. An example would be if a development required all homes to use specific material products or be in a particular square footage range.

House Specifications

Total living square footage is the heated square footage from outside the exterior framed walls; it doesn't include outdoor living areas, bonus rooms or garages. You'll need to calculate the approximate square footage of those areas to receive a close estimation of what your total construction cost will be. Don't forget that in most cases, a two-story home will cost less than a comparable one-story home of the same square footage, because there is less foundation and roofing.

As the homeowner, you'll be able to decide if you want to complete the bonus room with the rest of the house or wait. If you wait, find out what costs might be involved in demolition and retrofitting. It's also likely that you'll decide early on the rear deck/patio size. A pool, spa or outdoor kitchen will obviously add more costs to the total construction.

Materials

Product choice plays an important part in home affordability. You'll want to invest in good, low-maintenance exterior materials such as roof shingles and energy-efficient windows. You'll also want to include good insulation with high R-values, because all these items will save you money in the long run.

In product selection, you may need to decide between real stone or man-made stone veneers, or if you have a hillside walkout, you'll need to choose if you want to use brick or stucco veneer. Architectural features like copper gutters will increase construction costs. If you use a custom cabinetmaker, expect to pay more for your cabinetry.

Labor

The more materials you use that require specialists, the higher your costs. For example, if you use real stone, you'll pay for the services of a stone mason. You may eliminate some cost by applying sweat-equity; decide what you are comfortable doing, and leave the majority to the professionals. Because even if you have the know-how, you might not have the time, and that will only prolong your building schedule, costing you more money in the end.

Utilities

In regards to utilities, there are "hard costs" and monthly fees. A hard cost might be paying for the installation of a street lamp, and monthly fees are your operational costs. Think about what it will cost to prep your land for construction and occupancy. Depending upon where you build, you may have to drill a well instead of connecting to city water, or you might have to pay for a septic system.

Hopefully these ten principal factors – budget, financing, location, lot, permits/fees, land-use regulation, house specifications, materials, labor and utilities – will help you determine the affordability range for your new home. Gather as much information as you can about each aspect, and remember to keep your estimates updated. Figures can change yearly, quarterly or daily, and time may lapse from when you receive them to when you actually build.

Although it sounds like a lot of effort initially, doing your homework actually makes the experience more positive. You're less likely to be surprised by expenses and less likely to make choices that will send you over-budget. Just consider it as a fun type of adult "scavenger hunt," and get ready to start the next stage of your life!

Welcoming everything from major birthdays to historical events, the affordable homes in this section showcase distinctive architectural features, making use of ceiling heights and volume to increase living space. Many two-story ceilings and balconies connect the first and second floors, creating a sense of togetherness, while bay windows expand floor space, producing cozy nooks. Decorative ceilings and columns may even define rooms.

Milestones
significant events in life

Classic Craftsman Style

(Left) A clerestory captures the sky and places it under the cathedral ceiling, visually expanding space.
(Right) Cedar shake, brick and siding create an inviting Arts-n-Crafts exterior, a change the builder made to the original construction documents.
(Below) Wainscoting anchors the sunny breakfast nook.

© 2000 Donald A. Gardner, Inc.

The Hazelwood

❝I was standing by the counter, preparing a salad, when my husband closed his book, rose from the sofa, placed the volume on the mantel, calmly walked over to me and proudly stated he had just finished *War and Peace*. Reading that book was something he had wanted to do all of his life. I thought we should celebrate with more than a dinner salad.❞

Milestones
Donald A. Gardner Architects, Inc.

(Left) A tray ceiling and Tiffany-styled lighting fixture adds a touch of elegance to the dining room.

(Below) Inspired by work of Frank Lloyd Wright, this door features stained glass with a classic Craftsman feel.

(Right) Beaded board cabinetry visually connects the breakfast nook to the kitchen.

Stylish and sensible, this modest-size home makes the most of its square footage and lacks for nothing — not even a skylit bonus room for expansion. Taking the floor plan to new heights is a cathedral ceiling in the great room and tray ceilings in both the dining room and master bedroom. Triple windows are fashionable additions to the breakfast area and master bedroom, while a box bay window adds a special touch to the garage. The foyer opens to the great room and dining room, promoting easy gatherings.

The Hazelwood

1-800-388-7580

www.afforadablehomesforeverystageoflife.com

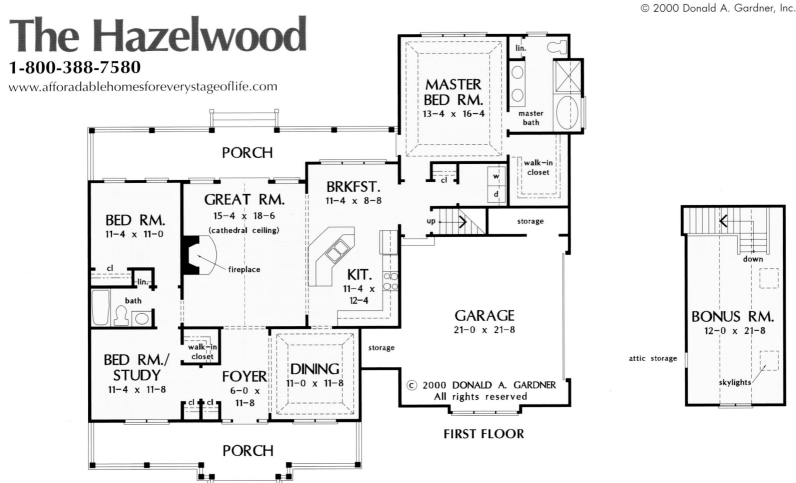

PORCH

MASTER BED RM.
13-4 x 16-4

lin.

master bath

walk-in closet

w d

cl

BRKFST.
11-4 x 8-8

GREAT RM.
15-4 x 18-6
(cathedral ceiling)

BED RM.
11-4 x 11-0

cl

lin.

bath

fireplace

KIT.
11-4 x 12-4

up

storage

BED RM./ STUDY
11-4 x 11-8

walk-in closet

FOYER
6-0 x 11-8

DINING
11-0 x 11-8

storage

GARAGE
21-0 x 21-8

cl cl

PORCH

FIRST FLOOR

down

BONUS RM.
12-0 x 21-8

attic storage

skylights

Affordable Homes • The Designs of Donald A. Gardner Architects, Inc.

A full-size bath is strategically located for easy accessibility from any part of the home. The master bath is a special haven complete with his-and-her lavatories, a garden tub and large shower. Note the spacious walk-in closet in the master suite, as well as the sizeable walk-in closet off the bedroom/study.

(Far Left) By changing the exterior building materials, this home now has the character of a home built in the 1930s.

(Left) With a modification, the homeowner chose to add a powder room by the front entrance.

(Below) Accent lighting enhances the crown molding, providing a subtle glow to the master bedroom.

Plan AHBDG01-884

- Total Living: 1724 s.f.
- Bonus Room: 329 s.f.
- 3 Bedrooms, 2 Baths
- Width: 62'4"
- Width: 57'10"
- Crawlspace Foundation
- Price Category C

Photographed home may have been modified from the original construction documents.

© 2000 Donald A. Gardner, Inc.

It was the night before the first day of kindergarten. Our daughter came into the master suite with tears in her eyes. She crawled in bed with us, and we all began to talk about the wonderful things she would learn. When she fell asleep, we put her to bed. The next morning she was excited about school, and we were the ones with tears in our eyes.

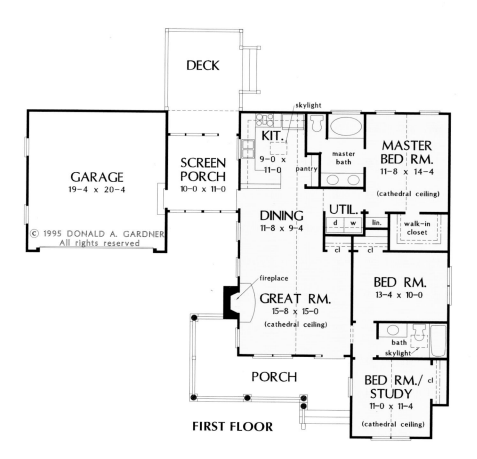

DECK

GARAGE
19-4 x 20-4

SCREEN
PORCH
10-0 x 11-0

KIT.
9-0 x 11-0

skylight

pantry

master bath

MASTER
BED RM.
11-8 x 14-4
(cathedral ceiling)

DINING
11-8 x 9-4

UTIL.
d   w   lin.

walk-in closet

cl   cl

fireplace

GREAT RM.
15-8 x 15-0
(cathedral ceiling)

BED RM.
13-4 x 10-0

bath
skylight

PORCH

BED RM./ cl
STUDY
11-0 x 11-4
(cathedral ceiling)

FIRST FLOOR

The Westport

1-800-388-7580
www.afforadablehomesforeverystageoflife.com

Plan AHBDG01-389

- Total Living: 1246 s.f.
- 3 Bedrooms, 2 Baths
- Width: 60'0"
- Depth: 48'0"
- Crawlspace Foundation
- Price Category B

Photographed home may have been modified from the original construction documents.

Milestones
Donald A. Gardner Architects, Inc.

ROCK SOLID
Design

(Left) Built-in cabinetry and a double-mantel fireplace create a stunning focal point in the great room.
(Right) Granite countertops and a tiled backsplash blend with clean-lined cabinetry for visual warmth.
(Below) Heavy crown molding accents the tray ceiling and wainscoting in the dining room.

The Satchwell

❝I didn't want a 30th birthday party, but I came home to a house full of people anyway. The dining room column was wrapped in streamers, and balloons billowed in the cathedral and tray ceilings. ❞

The Satchwell

1-800-388-7580

www.afforadablehomesforeverystageoflife.com

SCREEN PORCH
25-10 x 9-4

BRKFST.
11-8 x 8-10
(cathedral ceiling)

fireplace

GREAT RM.
19-0 x 15-8
(cathedral ceiling)

KIT.
11-8 x 12-4

bath

BED RM.
11-0 x 12-0

MASTER BED RM.
16-2 x 13-8

walk-in closet

walk-in closet

master bath

bath

cl

cl

FOYER
cl 6-0 x 11-0

DINING
11-0 x 13-0

UTIL.
6-0 x 10-4

up

w

d

down

BED RM.
11-8 x 11-8

BED RM./STUDY
11-4 x 12-10
(cathedral ceiling)

cl

PORCH

GARAGE
21-8 x 21-0

FIRST FLOOR

STORAGE

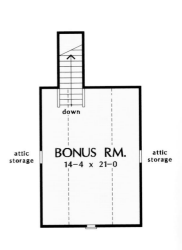

attic storage

BONUS RM.
14-4 x 21-0

attic storage

Affordable Homes • The Designs of Donald A. Gardner Architects, Inc.

Milestones
Donald A. Gardner Architects, Inc.

Graceful arches contrast with high gables for a stunning exterior on this Craftsman home. Windows with decorative transoms and several French doors flood the open floorplan with natural light. Decorative ceilings create visual space, while a screened porch allows for comfortable outdoor entertaining. Note the flexible bonus room and built-ins.

(**Far Left**) Stone correlates this Arts-n-Craft exterior to the natural surroundings.

(**Left**) A screened porch provides a nice spot for relaxation or entertaining.

(**Below Left**) The protruding breakfast nook is capped with a gabled roof.

(**Below**) A tray ceiling and rich golden walls are anchored by a decorative bed and heavy fabrics.

Plan AHBDG01-967

- Total Living: 2097 s.f.
- Bonus Room: 352 s.f.
- 4 Bedrooms, 3 Baths
- Width: 64'10"
- Width: 59'6"
- Crawlspace Foundation
- Price Category D

Photographed home may have been modified from the original construction documents.

SECOND FLOOR

MASTER BED RM.
13-10 x 14-0

skylights
master bath

walk-in closet

balcony

down

great room below

BED RM.
11-8 x 13-4

cl

lin.

bath

The MacLeish

1-800-388-7580

www.afforadablehomesforeverystageoflife.com

Plan AHBDG01-304

- Total Living: 1944 s.f.
- First Floor: 1271 s.f.
- Second Floor: 673 s.f.
- 4 Bedrooms, 3 Baths
- Width: 41'6"
- Depth: 44'8"
- Crawlspace Foundation
- Price Category C

Photographed home may have been modified from the original construction documents.

seat

spa

DECK

BRKFST.
12-10 x 7-6

PORCH

KITCHEN
15-0 x 7-10

BED RM.
11-8 x 10-4

DINING
13-4 x 12-0

cl

bath

balcony above

w

d

GREAT RM.
17-6 x 16-4

fireplace

up

© 1993 DONALD A. GARDNER
All rights reserved

cl

BED RM./
STUDY
11-8 x 12-8

PORCH

FIRST FLOOR

Modern COUNTRY

(Left) The angled granite counter reflects hints of the cabinetry's light stain.

(Right) The front porch creates a lovely outdoor living space, invoking the ambiance of times past.

(Below) With plenty of workspace for two cooks, the counter offers durability.

The Pennyhill

❝The movers finished packing the trucks, and I couldn't believe it. We were finally moving to our first house. When we drove up the driveway, it hit me. This was home. This was our home. My husband opened the front door. We walked into the empty great room, and the cathedral ceiling seemed to tower above us. Our laughter echoed as we walked through every room.❞

The Pennyhill

1-800-388-7580

www.afforadablehomesforeverystageoflife.com

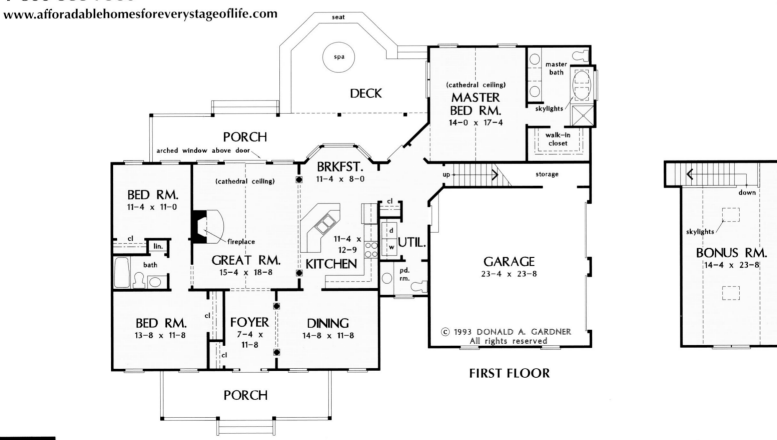

seat

spa

DECK

PORCH

arched window above door

(cathedral ceiling)
MASTER
BED RM.
14-0 x 17-4

master
bath

skylights

walk-in
closet

BED RM.
11-4 x 11-0

(cathedral ceiling)

BRKFST.
11-4 x 8-0

up   storage

cl

cl

lin.

fireplace

11-4 x
12-9

d
w

UTIL.

bath

GREAT RM.
15-4 x 18-8

KITCHEN

GARAGE
23-4 x 23-8

pd.
rm.

BED RM.
13-8 x 11-8

cl

FOYER
7-4 x
11-8

DINING
14-8 x 11-8

cl

PORCH

FIRST FLOOR

down

skylights

BONUS RM.
14-4 x 23-8

Affordable Homes • The Designs of Donald A. Gardner Architects, Inc.

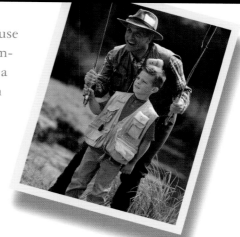

With porches and dormers, this house combines a quaint exterior with a contemporary, open floorplan. Featuring a central work counter, the kitchen is open to the great room. Located for privacy, the master suite includes a luxurious bath and walk-in closet. A bonus room provides extra space for a study, playroom or storage.

(Far Left) Low-maintenance siding reduces upkeep on this classic country design.
(Left) Adding casual elegance, the striking fireplace becomes the main focal point of the great room.

(Below Left) The rear façade showcases a large clerestory window.
(Below Right) A column helps define the dining room.

Plan AHBDG01-294

- Total Living: 1864 s.f.
- Bonus Room: 420 s.f.
- 3 Bedrooms, 2-1/2 Baths
- Width: 71'0"
- Depth: 56'4"
- Crawlspace Foundation
- Price Category C

photographed home may have been modified from the original construction documents.

© 1993 Donald A. Gardner Architects, Inc.

As we neared retirement age, we decided to sell everything and build a smaller, low-maintenance home. It's just the right size for the two of us, and there's room for guests.

The Portland

Plan AHBDG01-897

- Total Living: 1488 s.f.
- Bonus Room: 397 s.f.
- 3 Bedrooms, 2 Baths
- Width: 53'4"
- Depth: 59'8"
- Crawlspace Foundation
- Price Category B

1-800-388-7580
www.affordablehomesforeverystageoflife.com

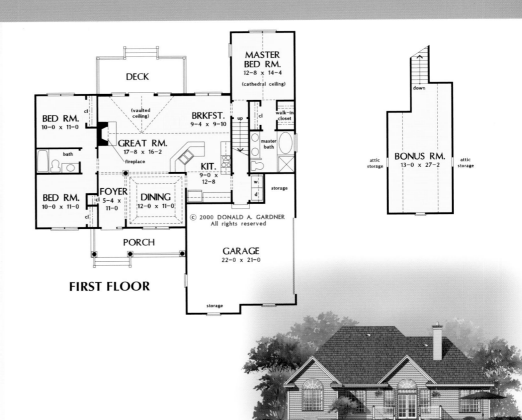

FIRST FLOOR

DECK

BED RM. 10-0 x 11-0

(vaulted ceiling)

GREAT RM. 17-8 x 16-2

fireplace

bath

FOYER 5-4 x 11-0

DINING 12-0 x 11-0

BED RM. 10-0 x 11-0

PORCH

BRKFST. 9-4 x 9-10

KIT. 9-0 x 12-8

MASTER BED RM. 12-8 x 14-4 (cathedral ceiling)

up

walk-in closet

master bath

storage

GARAGE 22-0 x 21-0

storage

down

BONUS RM. 13-0 x 27-2

attic storage

attic storage

REAR ELEVATION

ur daughter spent the night with us last night. She came into the kitchen for coffee when we realized she's starting another chapter in her life. She's getting married today.

© 1997 Donald A. Gardner Architects, Inc.

The Anniston

Plan AHBDG01-540

- Total Living: 1652 s.f.
- Bonus Room: 367 s.f.
- 3 Bedrooms, 2 Baths
- Width: 64'4"
- Depth: 51'0"
- Crawlspace Foundation
- Price Category C

1-800-388-7580
www.affordablehomesforeverystageoflife.com

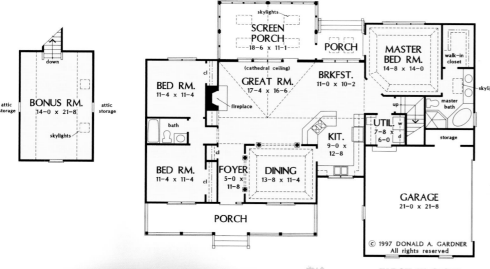

FIRST FLOOR

REAR ELEVATION © 1997 Donald A. Gardner Architects, Inc.

Donald A. Gardner Architects, Inc.

The last payment on our house did it. We are officially debt free — no credit card bills, no car payments — just the monthly bills. Now we're going to remodel the bonus room.

The Delaney

Plan AHBDG01-502

- Total Living: 1521 s.f.
- Bonus Room: 283 s.f.
- 3 Bedrooms, 2 Baths
- Width: 51'10"
- Depth: 55'4"
- Crawlspace Foundation
- Price Category C

1-800-388-7580
www.affordablehomesforeverystageoflife.com

FIRST FLOOR

BRKFST. 9-0 x 9-0
PATIO
BED RM. 11-0 x 11-0
KIT. 9-0 x 9-6
GREAT RM. 16-2 x 16-2
MASTER BED RM. 12-0 x 14-0
bath
fireplace (cathedral ceiling)
UTIL. 6-0 x 11-0
DINING 11-0 x 12-4
FOYER 6-4 x 8-4
master bath
BED RM. 11-0 x 11-0
walk-in closet
PORCH
GARAGE 21-8 x 21-0

down
attic storage
attic storage
BONUS RM. 12-8 x 21-0
skylights

REAR ELEVATION

My wife has used the bedroom/study more than any room in the house. Now that she's passed the State Bar, I'm hoping she'll be able to relax in the great room more often.

The Henderson

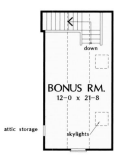

BONUS RM.
12–0 x 21–8

attic storage

skylights

down

skylight

MASTER BED RM.
13–4 x 16–4

master bath

lin.

walk-in closet

w. d

storage

PORCH

BED RM.
11–4 x 11–0

GREAT RM.
15–4 x 18–6
(cathedral ceiling)

fireplace

BRKFST.
11–4 x 8–8

cl

up

KIT.
11–4 x 12–10

GARAGE
21–0 x 21–8

storage

cl

lin.

bath

walk-in closet

BED RM./ STUDY
11–0 x 11–8

FOYER
6–0 x 8–4

DINING
11–0 x 11–8

© 1996 DONALD A. GARDNER
All rights reserved

PORCH

FIRST FLOOR

Plan AHBDG01-439

- Total Living: 1685 s.f.
- Bonus Room: 331 s.f.
- 3 Bedrooms, 2 Baths
- Width: 62'4"
- Width: 57'4"
- Crawlspace Foundation
- Price Category C

1-800-388-7580
www.affordablehomesforeverystageoflife.com

REAR ELEVATION © 1996 Donald A. Gardner Architects, Inc.

Donald A. Gardner Architects, Inc.

35

A fter my son won the championship, he came home and arranged the shelves in his room for an hour or so, looking for the perfect place for his trophy.

The Armond

Plan AHBDG01-989

- Total Living: 1654 s.f.
- Bonus Room: 356 s.f.
- 3 Bedrooms, 2 Baths
- Width: 60'4"
- Depth: 47'10"
- Crawlspace Foundation
- Price Category C

1-800-388-7580

www.affordablehomesforeverystageoflife.com

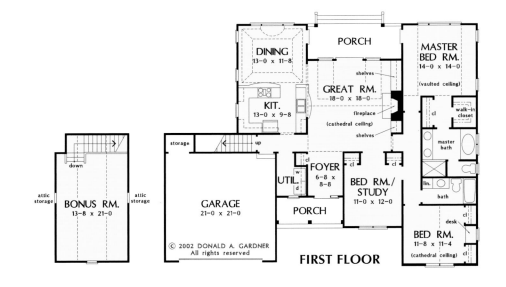

After battling an illness for some time, my wife finally won. She returned from the hospital to find a house full of friends and family, along with a master suite full of roses.

© 2003 Donald A. Gardner, Inc.

The Jarrel

BONUS RM.
13-4 x 22-0

attic storage

down

SCREEN PORCH
17-8 x 10-0

DINING
11-0 x 12-4

MASTER BED RM.
16-4 x 14-8

walk-in closet

linen

KIT.
11-0 x 12-4
(cathedral ceiling)

fireplace

GREAT RM.
17-2 x 19-4
(cathedral ceiling)

master bath

seat

bath

cabinets

coats

FOYER
7-4 x 6-8

BEDROOM/ STUDY
11-0 x 12-4

UTIL.

w
d

up

BED RM.
11-0 x 12-4

PORCH

GARAGE
21-0 x 22-0

© 2003 DONALD A. GARDNER
All rights reserved

FIRST FLOOR

Plan AHBDG01-1017

- Total Living: 1727 s.f.
- Bonus Room: 346 s.f.
- 3 Bedrooms, 2 Baths
- Width: 46'0"
- Depth: 66'4"
- Crawlspace Foundation
- Price Category C

1-800-388-7580
www.affordablehomesforeverystageoflife.com

Donald A. Gardner Architects, Inc.

37

REAR ELEVATION
© 2003 Donald A. Gardner, Inc.

When my husband arrived home, there was a candlelit dinner awaiting him in the dining room. He had just completed his residency, and we were celebrating the next step.

The Barrymore

Plan AHBDG01-982

- Total Living: 1606 s.f.
- Bonus Room: 338 s.f.
- 3 Bedrooms, 2 Baths
- Width: 50'0"
- Depth: 54'0"
- Crawlspace Foundation
- Price Category C

1-800-388-7580
www.affordablehomesforeverystageoflife.com

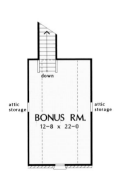

FIRST FLOOR

Who would have thought I would become a writer after I retired — much less have my first book published? The back porch and breakfast nook have proven to be places of inspiration.

The Jonesboro

Plan AHBDG01-983

- Total Living: 1700 s.f.
- Bonus Room: 333 s.f.
- 3 Bedrooms, 2 Baths
- Width: 49'0"
- Depth: 65'4"
- Crawlspace Foundation
- Price Category C

1-800-388-7580
www.affordablehomesforeverystageoflife.com

FIRST FLOOR

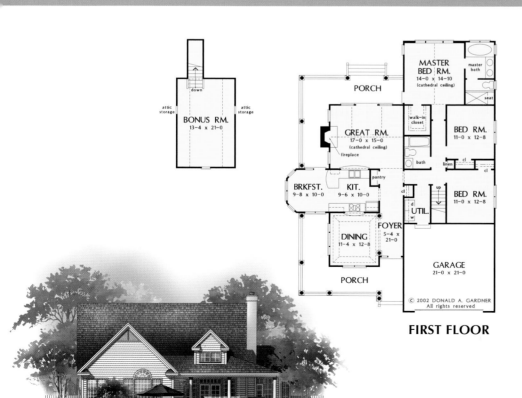

REAR ELEVATION

Donald A. Gardner Architects, Inc.

After we finished dinner, my daughter helped me clear the table, while her boyfriend talked to her father in the great room. He asked my husband for her hand in marriage!

The Jennings

Plan AHBDG01-386

- Total Living: 1512 s.f.
- 3 Bedrooms, 2 Baths
- Width: 64'4"
- Depth: 44'4"
- Crawlspace Foundation
- Price Category C

1-800-388-7580
www.affordablehomesforeverystageoflife.com

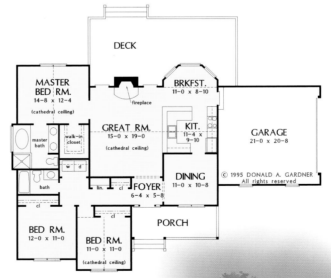

FIRST FLOOR

Affordable Homes

REAR ELEVATION

A fter graduation, we had a get-together at our house. My son was on the deck in his gown when he saw me through the bay and blew me a kiss.

© 1995 Donald A. Gardner Architects, Inc.

The Liberty Hill

FIRST FLOOR

SECOND FLOOR

Plan AHBDG01-414

- Total Living: 1883 s.f.
- First Floor: 1803 s.f.
- Second Floor: 80 s.f.
- Bonus Room: 918 s.f.
- 3 Bedrooms, 2 Baths
- Width: 63'8"
- Depth: 57'4"
- Crawlspace Foundation
- Price Category C

1-800-388-7580
www.affordablehomesforeverystageoflife.com

Donald A. Gardner Architects, Inc.

41

REAR ELEVATION © 1995 Donald A. Gardner Architects, Inc.

My wife's mission is to wipe out adult illiteracy. She tutors a number of individuals in our study. It's amazing how learning to read changes their lives, and how their lives change ours.

© 2003 Donald A. Gardner, Inc.

The Hilligan

Plan AHBDG01-1015

- Total Living: 1535 s.f.
- Bonus Room: 355 s.f.
- 3 Bedrooms, 2 Baths
- Width: 59'8"
- Depth: 47'4"
- Crawlspace Foundation
- Price Category C

1-800-388-7580
www.affordablehomesforeverystageoflife.com

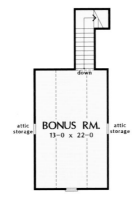

BONUS RM.
13-0 x 22-0

attic storage · attic storage

down

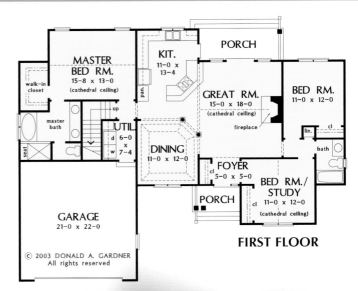

MASTER BED RM.
15-8 x 13-0
(cathedral ceiling)

walk-in closet

master bath

seat

KIT.
11-0 x 13-4

pan.

up

UTIL.
d 6-0 x w 7-4

DINING
11-0 x 12-0

PORCH

GREAT RM.
15-0 x 18-0
(cathedral ceiling)

fireplace

BED RM.
11-0 x 12-0

lin. · cl

bath

FOYER
5-0 x 5-0

PORCH

BED RM./ STUDY
11-0 x 12-0
(cathedral ceiling)

GARAGE
21-0 x 22-0

© 2003 DONALD A. GARDNER
All rights reserved

FIRST FLOOR

REAR ELEVATION   © 2003 Donald A. Gardner, Inc.

Paying off our student loans was quite an accomplishment for us. So we decided to build a second home in the mountains. We loved the Arts-n-Crafts character of this plan.

© 2000 Donald A. Gardner, Inc.

The Kirkaldie

FIRST FLOOR

REAR ELEVATION   © 2000 Donald A. Gardner, Inc.

Plan AHBDG01-901

- Total Living: 1684 s.f.
- 3 Bedrooms, 2 Baths
- Width: 53'4"
- Depth: 66'10"
- Crawlspace Foundation
- Price Category C

1-800-388-7580
www.affordablehomesforeverystageoflife.com

Donald A. Gardner Architects, Inc.

She arrived late, went to her bedroom and shortly thereafter came into the dining room where we were eating, proudly displaying her voter registration card. Oh, the wonders of turning 18!

© 2000 Donald A. Gardner, Inc.

The Dunloring

Plan AHBDG01-872

- Total Living: 1682 s.f.
- 3 Bedrooms, 2-1/2 Baths
- Width: 48'4"
- Depth: 64'0"
- Crawlspace Foundation
- Price Category C

1-800-388-7580
www.affordablehomesforeverystageoflife.com

MASTER BED RM.
13-4 x 15-8

master bath

PORCH

DINING
12-0 x 13-0

walk-in closet

seat

fireplace

GREAT RM.
19-0 x 17-4
(cathedral ceiling)

KITCHEN
12-0 x 11-0

BED RM.
12-4 x 11-0

cl

cl

cl

cl

cl

bath

d
w

UTIL.

storage

pd. rm.

FOYER
8-0 x 8-4
(10' ceiling)

BED RM./ STUDY
12-8 x 12-0
(10' ceiling)

PORCH

GARAGE
21-0 x 21-0

FIRST FLOOR

REAR ELEVATION

As if the year 2000 wasn't significant enough, it was the same year we built our vacation house. We gave the kids their own area by converting the bonus room into a playroom.

The Tolliver

Plan AHBDG01-859

- Total Living: 1228 s.f.
- Bonus Room: 444 s.f.
- 3 Bedrooms, 2 Baths
- Width: 47'0"
- Depth: 40'4"
- Crawlspace Foundation
- Price Category B

1-800-388-7580
www.affordablehomesforeverystageoflife.com

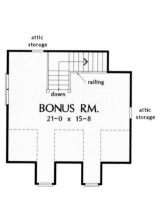

BONUS RM.
21-0 x 15-8

attic storage

attic storage

railing

down

walk-in closet

MASTER BED RM.
14-0 x 11-0
(cathedral ceiling)

master bath

BED RM.
11-0 x 11-0

BED RM.
11-4 x 11-0

cl

cl

up

bath

lin.

pan.

d   w

GARAGE
21-0 x 21-0

KIT.
11-0 x 9-4

GREAT RM.
13-8 x 16-0
(cathedral ceiling)
fireplace

© 2000 DONALD A. GARDNER
All rights reserved

DINING
11-0 x 12-0

PORCH

FIRST FLOOR

Our son was at the table in the breakfast nook, doing his homework, when he asked us what major historical events had changed our lives. The moon landing and Vietnam War were mentioned.

The Cleveland

Plan AHBDG01-412

- Total Living: 1633 s.f.
- Bonus Room: 595 s.f.
- 3 Bedrooms, 2 Baths
- Width: 65'4"
- Depth: 46'0"
- Crawlspace Foundation
- Price Category C

1-800-388-7580
www.affordablehomesforeverystageoflife.com

FIRST FLOOR

DECK

MASTER BED RM.
14-8 x 13-4
(cathedral ceiling)

BRKFST.
11-0 x 9-5

fireplace

master bath

walk-in closet

GREAT RM.
16-0 x 19-0
(cathedral ceiling)

KIT.
11-4 x 10-7

GARAGE
21-0 x 23-4

w d
UTIL.

balcony above up

bath

lin.

BED RM.
12-0 x 11-0

BED RM./ STUDY
11-0 x 12-0
(cathedral ceiling)

FOYER
7-4 x 5-8

DINING
11-0 x 12-4

PORCH

SECOND FLOOR

BONUS
14-8 x 17-0
(unfinished)

great room below

down

railing

balcony (optional)

BONUS
11-0 x 12-4
(unfinished)

attic storage

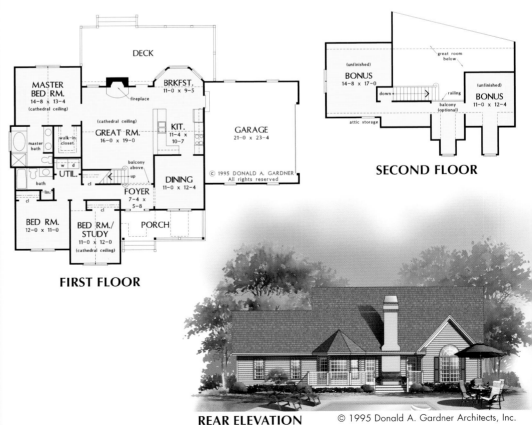

REAR ELEVATION

For our 25th anniversary present to each other, we decided to build a vacation house at the lake. Now we spend all of our weekends there, and sometimes our grandbaby comes along.

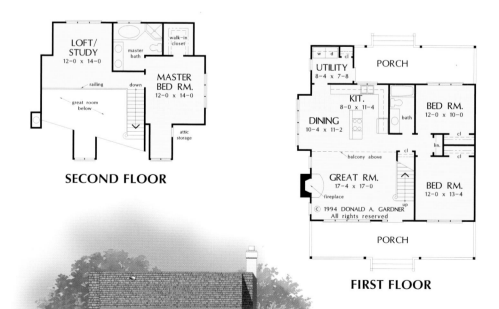

The Meredith

Plan AHBDG01-355

- Total Living: 1694 s.f.
- First Floor: 1100 s.f.
- Second Floor: 594 s.f.
- 3 Bedrooms, 2 Baths
- Width: 36'8"
- Depth: 45'0"
- Crawlspace Foundation
- Price Category C

1-800-388-7580
www.affordablehomesforeverystageoflife.com

SECOND FLOOR

LOFT/STUDY 12-0 x 14-0
master bath
walk-in closet
railing
down
great room below
MASTER BED RM. 12-0 x 14-0
attic storage

FIRST FLOOR

w d cl
UTILITY 8-4 x 7-8
PORCH
KIT. 8-0 x 11-4
DINING 10-4 x 11-2
bath
BED RM. 12-0 x 10-0
cl
lin.
cl
balcony above
GREAT RM. 17-4 x 17-0
fireplace
© 1994 DONALD A. GARDNER All rights reserved
cl
up
BED RM. 12-0 x 13-4
PORCH

Donald A. Gardner Architects, Inc.

47

Our life changed when our son went to college. The house was quieter. There was more food in the refrigerator, and we could watch whatever we wanted in the home theatre.

The Alden

Plan AHBDG01-957

- Total Living: 1898 s.f.
- Bonus Room: 416 s.f.
- 3 Bedrooms, 2 Baths
- Width: 66'0"
- Depth: 60'0"
- Crawlspace Foundation
- Price Category C

1-800-388-7580
www.affordablehomesforeverystageoflife.com

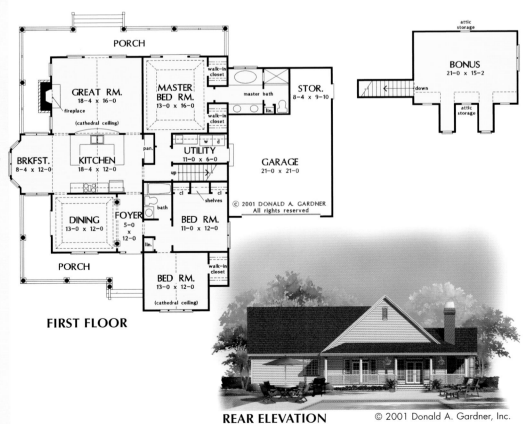

FIRST FLOOR

REAR ELEVATION

She's sweet sixteen and going to her first prom. She's used the whole house as her catwalk, modeling her gown for everyone. She even found her dad out in the garage.

The Riverbirch

FIRST FLOOR

Plan AHBDG01-782

- Total Living: 1733 s.f.
- Bonus Room: 372 s.f.
- 3 Bedrooms, 2 Baths
- Width: 65'8"
- Depth: 49'8"
- Crawlspace Foundation
- Price Category C

1-800-388-7580
www.affordablehomesforeverystageoflife.com

REAR ELEVATION

Donald A. Gardner Architects, Inc.

fter our company won a "Best In State" award, we received a lot more business — enough to build our home with the attention to detail and products we desired.

© 1998 Donald A. Gardner, Inc.

The Raintree

Plan AHBDG01-721

- Total Living: 1762 s.f.
- Bonus Room: 316 s.f.
- 3 Bedrooms, 2 Baths
- Width: 56'8"
- Depth: 59'0"
- Crawlspace Foundation
- Price Category C

1-800-388-7580

www.affordablehomesforeverystageoflife.com

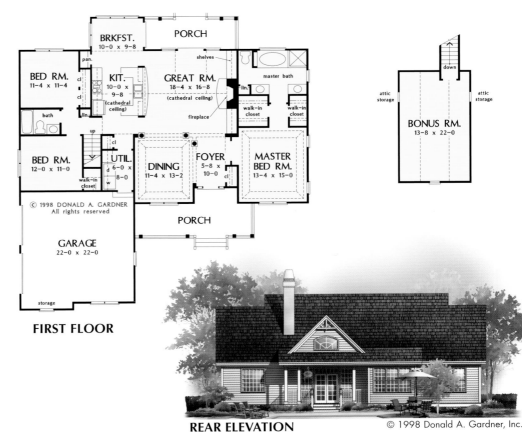

FIRST FLOOR

BRKFST. 10-0 x 9-8

PORCH

BED RM. 11-4 x 11-4

KIT. 10-0 x 9-8 (cathedral ceiling)

GREAT RM. 18-4 x 16-8 (cathedral ceiling)

shelves

master bath

walk-in closet

walk-in closet

fireplace

bath

up

UTIL. d 6-0 x w 8-0

DINING 11-4 x 13-2

FOYER 5-8 x 10-0

MASTER BED RM. 13-4 x 15-0

BED RM. 12-0 x 11-0

walk-in closet

© 1998 DONALD A. GARDNER All rights reserved

PORCH

GARAGE 22-0 x 22-0

storage

BONUS RM. 13-8 x 22-0

attic storage

attic storage

down

REAR ELEVATION

© 1998 Donald A. Gardner, Inc.

I conquered my fear of heights when we built our house on top of a steep hill. The views from our porches are just too breathtaking to allow myself to be frightened.

The Sunderland

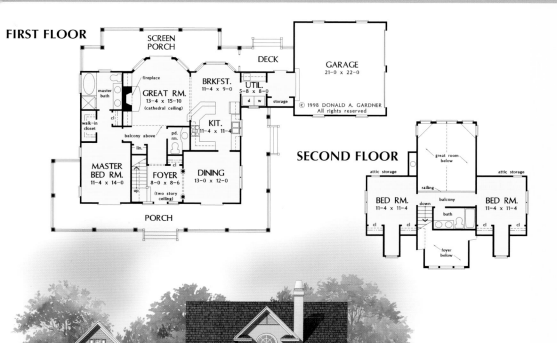

FIRST FLOOR

SECOND FLOOR

PORCH

Plan AHBDG01-545

- Total Living: 1761 s.f.
- First Floor: 1271 s.f.
- Second Floor: 490 s.f.
- 3 Bedrooms, 2-1/2 Baths
- Width: 77'8"
- Depth: 50'0"
- Crawlspace Foundation
- Price Category C

1-800-388-7580
www.affordablehomesforeverystageoflife.com

REAR ELEVATION

Donald A. Gardner Architects, Inc.

Welcoming everything from extended family households to volunteering, the affordable homes in this section implement natural traffic flows. With circular and branch configurations, the traffic patterns complement both open and more traditionally defined floorplans. Natural traffic flows help make homes more family-efficient, and family-efficiency means a better quality of life.

Transitions
going from place to place to place

Colorful
Contemporary

(Far Left) Mimicking a Palladian window, an opening tops two stately columns, brightening the great room.

(Right) A pocket-door with frosted glass connects the kitchen to the dining room.

(Below) An angled counter is all that separates the kitchen from the breakfast nook.

The Hampton

"One year we participated in the foreign exchange student program. Our daughter went to Spain and a student from Spain came to live with us. She moved into our daughter's bedroom and into our lives. It was such a joy to have her share her customs and to show her ours. Even though she's back in her home country, we still keep in touch."

Transitions
Donald A. Gardner Architects, Inc.

(**Left**) A barrel-vault arch and circle-head transom top the dining room's large picture window.
(**Below**) The bonus room was transformed into a home office that receives clients.
(**Right**) A cathedral ceiling, clerestory window and built-in cabinetry highlight the great room.

Dormers cast light and interest into the foyer for a grand first impression that sets the tone in a home full of today's amenities. The great room, articulated by columns, features a cathedral ceiling and is conveniently located adjacent to the breakfast room and kitchen. Tray ceilings and picture windows with circle tops accent the front bedroom and dining room.

The Hampton

1-800-388-7580

www.afforadablehomesforeverystageoflife.com

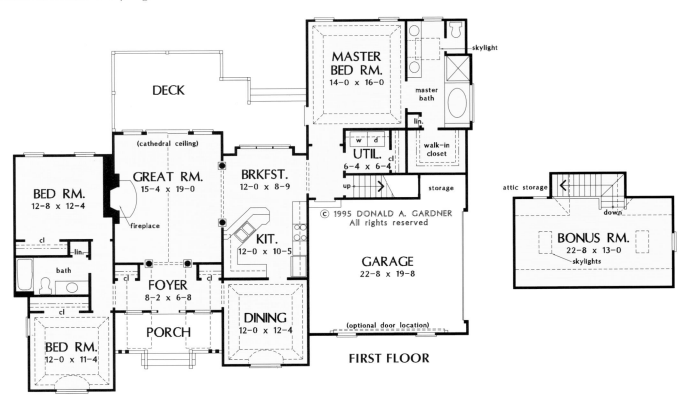

DECK

BED RM.
12-8 x 12-4

GREAT RM.
15-4 x 19-0

(cathedral ceiling)

fireplace

cl

lin.

bath

cl

BED RM.
12-0 x 11-4

FOYER
8-2 x 6-8

cl

PORCH

BRKFST.
12-0 x 8-9

KIT.
12-0 x 10-5

DINING
12-0 x 12-4

MASTER BED RM.
14-0 x 16-0

skylight

master bath

lin.

walk-in closet

w   d

UTIL.
6-4 x 6-4

cl

up

storage

GARAGE
22-8 x 19-8

(optional door location)

FIRST FLOOR

attic storage

down

BONUS RM.
22-8 x 13-0

skylights

Affordable Homes • The Designs of Donald A. Gardner Architects, Inc.

Transitions
Donald A. Gardner Architects, Inc.

A secluded master suite, highlighted by a tray ceiling in the bedroom, includes a bath with skylight, garden tub, separate shower, double bowl vanity and spacious walk-in closet.

(Far Left) Twin dormers and gables add symmetrical balance to the porch.
(Left) A large mirror makes the spacious master bath seem even larger.
(Below Left) French doors and windows usher in the light and views.
(Below) Cool gray walls and clean-lined furniture create a tranquil master suite.

Plan AHBDG01-390

- Total Living: 1879 s.f.
- Bonus Room: 360 s.f.
- 3 Bedrooms, 2 Baths
- Width: 66'4"
- Depth: 55'2"
- Crawlspace Foundation
- Price Category C

Photographed home may have been modified from the original construction documents.

© 1995 Donald A. Gardner Architects, Inc.

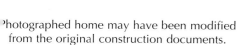

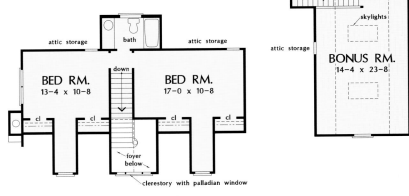

> We had a family meeting in the dining room and discussed how opening a business would change our lives. We talked of sacrifices and rewards. With everyone's support, my wife and I proceeded the next day. We converted the bonus room into an office within a week and began the preliminaries soon after. It's been about two years now, and business is great. "

SECOND FLOOR

The Glenwood

1-800-388-7580

www.afforadablehomesforeverystageoflife.com

Plan AHBDG01-224

- Total Living: 1831 s.f.
- First Floor: 1289 s.f.
- Second Floor: 542 s.f.
- Bonus Room: 393 s.f.
- 3 Bedrooms, 2-1/2 Baths
- Width: 66'4"
- Depth: 40'4"
- Crawlspace Foundation
- Price Category C

Photographed home may have been modified from the original construction documents.

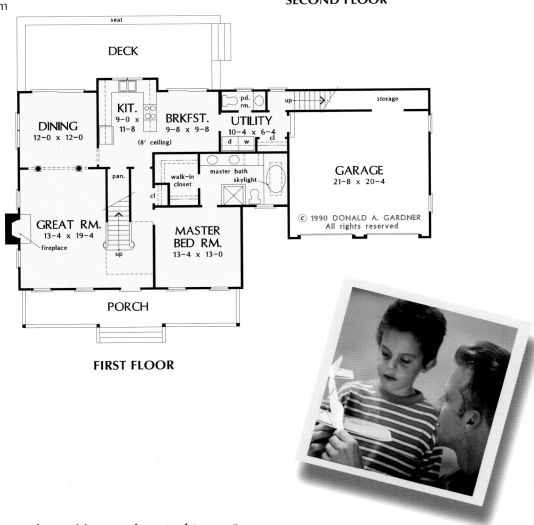

FIRST FLOOR

Quaint Curbside Appeal

(**Left**) Framing the sky, a large clerestory window towers above French doors, creating an airy great room.

(**Right**) A column and chair-rail accent the formal dining room.

(**Below**) Providing a shady spot for warm days, the expansive porch captures fresh breezes.

The Stratford

" We didn't take adopting a pet lightly. After months of begging from our son, we purchased the necessary supplies, chose a dog from the humane society and enrolled our dog in puppy kindergarten. Our son takes the dog to every class. The puppy is learning simple commands. Our son is learning responsibility, and our home has a wonderful new family member. "

The Stratford

1-800-388-7580

www.afforadablehomesforeverystageoflife.com

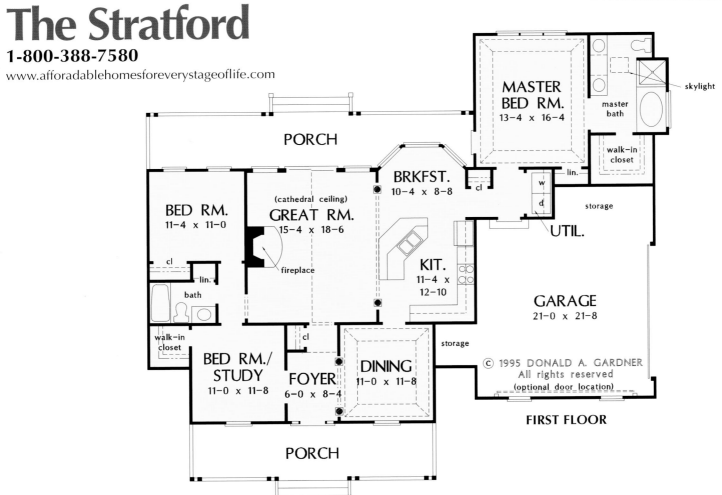

FIRST FLOOR

PORCH

MASTER BED RM.
13-4 x 16-4

master bath

skylight

walk-in closet

lin.

BRKFST.
10-4 x 8-8

cl

w
d

storage

UTIL.

BED RM.
11-4 x 11-0

(cathedral ceiling)
GREAT RM.
15-4 x 18-6

fireplace

cl

lin.

bath

walk-in closet

KIT.
11-4 x 12-10

GARAGE
21-0 x 21-8

BED RM./
STUDY
11-0 x 11-8

FOYER
6-0 x 8-4

cl

DINING
11-0 x 11-8

storage

PORCH

Transitions
Donald A. Gardner Architects, Inc.

From its wide front porch to its front bedroom/study, this home has the extras today's families want. With its openness and efficient use of space, the floorplan maximizes square footage. The great room features clerestory windows, a cathedral ceiling and French doors that access a porch. The master suite is designed to pamper.

(Far Left) With low-maintenance siding and columns, this charmer possesses curb appeal.
(Left) Along with providing a breakfast bar, the kitchen's island counter services the great room.
(Below Left) As inviting from the rear exterior as it is from the front, the back features striking glasswork.

(Below) A tray ceiling adds elegance to the cool blue master bedroom.

Plan AHBDG01-384

- Total Living: 1632 s.f.
- 3 Bedrooms, 2 Baths
- Width: 62'4"
- Depth: 55'2"
- Crawlspace Foundation
- Price Category C

Photographed home may have been modified from the original construction documents.

"My husband is a regional manager, so we literally live in two states. We spend about two weeks a month in each state. For our toddler and me, it's almost like taking a vacation twice a month. We especially love this house, because it overlooks a lake. I telecommute, so I work from the deck when our toddler plays outside."

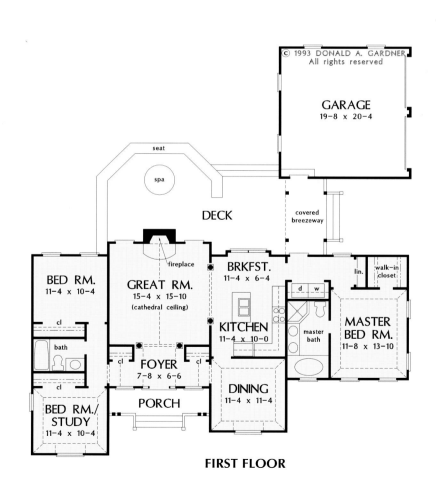

GARAGE
19-8 x 20-4

seat

spa

DECK

covered breezeway

fireplace

BRKFST.
11-4 x 6-4

lin.

walk-in closet

BED RM.
11-4 x 10-4

GREAT RM.
15-4 x 15-10
(cathedral ceiling)

cl

bath

cl

FOYER
7-8 x 6-6

cl

KITCHEN
11-4 x 10-0

d w

master bath

MASTER
BED RM.
11-8 x 13-10

cl

BED RM./
STUDY
11-4 x 10-4

PORCH

DINING
11-4 x 11-4

FIRST FLOOR

The Preston
1-800-388-7580
www.afforadablehomesforeverystageoflife.com

Plan AHBDG01-322

- Total Living: 1452 s.f.
- 3 Bedrooms, 2 Baths
- Width: 58'0"
- Depth: 35'8"
- Crawlspace Foundation
- Price Category B

Photographed home may have been modified from the original construction documents.

Transitions
Donald A. Gardner Architects, Inc.

We finished building our house in time for the town's first annual Fall Festival. Our house is within walking distance to the festivities, so we adorned our house with seasonal decorations.

© 2002 Donald A. Gardner, Inc.

The Irby

Plan AHBDG01-993

- Total Living: 1580 s.f.
- Bonus Room: 367 s.f.
- 3 Bedrooms, 2 Baths
- Width: 55'6"
- Depth: 46'0"
- Crawlspace Foundation
- Price Category C

1-800-388-7580
www.affordablehomesforeverystageoflife.com

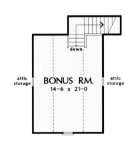

REAR ELEVATION © 2002 Donald A. Gardner, Inc.

s I prepared for my first marathon, our guest bedroom was turned into a home gym. Our property became my training track; seven laps around it equals one mile.

The Gentry

FIRST FLOOR

DECK
18-8 x 8-0

fireplace

GREAT RM.
18-0 x 17-4
(cathedral ceiling)

KITCHEN
13-0 x 10-0

BRKFST.
9-0 x 10-0

PORCH

MASTER
BED RM.
13-0 x 17-4

shelves

BED RM.
12-0 x 11-0

walk-in
closet

lin.

master
bath

FOYER
6-0 x
12-8

DINING
13-0 x 12-8

bath

lin.

cl

cl

UTILITY
6-0 x
11-0

up

d

w

BED RM.
12-0 x 11-0

PORCH

sto.

GARAGE
22-0 x 21-0

sto.

down

attic
storage

attic
storage

BONUS RM.
14-4 x 23-4

Plan AHBDG01-977

- Total Living: 1827 s.f.
- Bonus Room: 384 s.f.
- 3 Bedrooms, 2 Baths
- Width: 61'8"
- Depth: 62'8"
- Crawlspace Foundation
- Price Category C

1-800-388-7580
www.affordablehomesforeverystageoflife.com

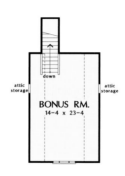

REAR ELEVATION

Donald A. Gardner Architects, Inc.

Life sometimes throws a curve ball; I understood what that meant when I became a single parent. This home was just perfect for my children and me.

The Northslope

Plan AHBDG01-797

- Total Living: 1481 s.f.
- Bonus Room: 643 s.f.
- 3 Bedrooms, 2 Baths
- Width: 42'4"
- Depth: 65'10"
- Crawlspace Foundation
- Price Category B

1-800-388-7580
www.affordablehomesforeverystageoflife.com

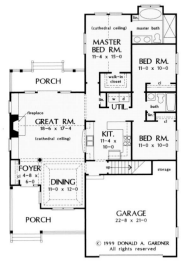

FIRST FLOOR

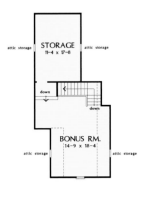

REAR ELEVATION   © 1999 Donald A. Gardner, Inc.

Moving from the city to the country was a huge adjustment at first, but now we look through the great room windows every morning and can't imagine living anywhere else.

The Carriageparke

Plan AHBDG01-758

- Total Living: 1460 s.f.
- 3 Bedrooms, 2 Baths
- Width: 54'8"
- Depth: 46'8"
- Crawlspace Foundation
- Price Category B

1-800-388-7580
www.affordablehomesforeverystageoflife.com

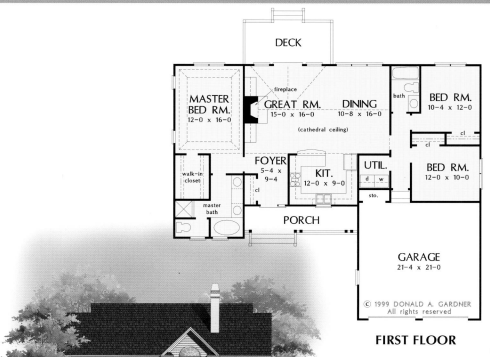

DECK

MASTER BED RM.
12-0 x 16-0

fireplace

GREAT RM.
15-0 x 16-0

DINING
10-8 x 16-0

(cathedral ceiling)

bath

BED RM.
10-4 x 12-0

cl

cl

walk-in closet

FOYER
5-4 x 9-4

KIT.
12-0 x 9-0

UTIL.

d   w

BED RM.
12-0 x 10-0

sto.

master bath

cl

PORCH

GARAGE
21-4 x 21-0

FIRST FLOOR

REAR ELEVATION

Donald A. Gardner Architects, Inc.

fter I received a promotion, we were able to save for a vacation house. We choose to build this design, because it blends with the vernacular of our mountain lot.

The Sherbrooke

Plan AHBDG01-902

- Total Living: 1854 s.f.
- 3 Bedrooms, 2-1/2 Baths
- Width: 56'0"
- Depth: 73'0"
- Crawlspace Foundation
- Price Category C

1-800-388-7580
www.affordablehomesforeverystageoflife.com

FIRST FLOOR

O ur son informed us that he was joining the ranks of the "boomerang children" — those that return home after college. His return was an adjustment, because he is neater than we are!

The Elmhurst

Plan AHBDG01-886

- Total Living: 1974 s.f.
- First Floor: 1471 s.f.
- Second Floor: 503 s.f.
- Bonus Room: 277 s.f.
- 3 Bedrooms, 2-1/2 Baths
- Width: 59'0"
- Depth: 50'4"
- Crawlspace Foundation
- Price Category C

1-800-388-7580
www.affordablehomesforeverystageoflife.com

Donald A. Gardner Architects, Inc.

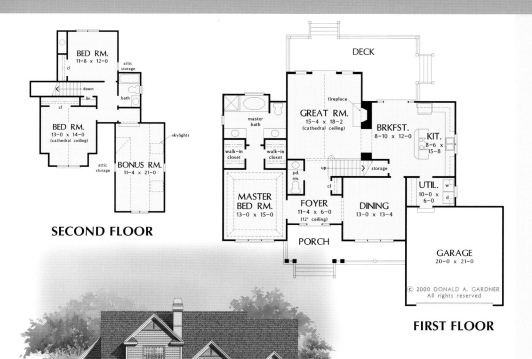

SECOND FLOOR

BED RM.
11–8 x 12–0

attic storage

bath

down

lin.

cl

BED RM.
13–0 x 14–0
(cathedral ceiling)

skylights

BONUS RM.
11–4 x 21–0

attic storage

DECK

fireplace

GREAT RM.
15–4 x 18–2
(cathedral ceiling)

BRKFST.
8–10 x 12–0

KIT.
8–6 x 15–8

master bath

walk-in closet

walk-in closet

up

storage

pd. rm.

cl

UTIL.
10–0 x 6–0

w
d

MASTER BED RM.
13–0 x 15–0

FOYER
11–4 x 6–0
(12' ceiling)

DINING
13–0 x 13–4

PORCH

GARAGE
20–0 x 21–0

FIRST FLOOR

REAR ELEVATION

In the ten years since we built this house, we have watched this town turn into a little city. Although it's growing, it still hasn't lost its small-town charm.

The Morninglory

Plan AHBDG01-236

- Total Living: 1778 s.f.
- First Floor: 1325 s.f.
- Second Floor: 453 s.f.
- 3 Bedrooms, 2-1/2 Baths
- Width: 48'4"
- Depth: 40'4"
- Crawlspace Foundation
- Price Category C

1-800-388-7580
www.affordablehomesforeverystageoflife.com

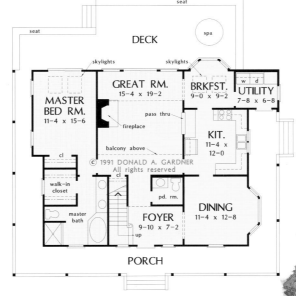

FIRST FLOOR

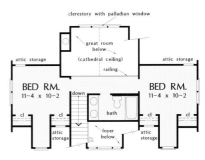

SECOND FLOOR

REAR ELEVATION   © 1991 Donald A. Gardner Architects, Ir

When my son went pro, my first gift was a new car. The second gift was this house; it's just the right size for me, and it's filled with all the latest amenities.

The Edelweiss

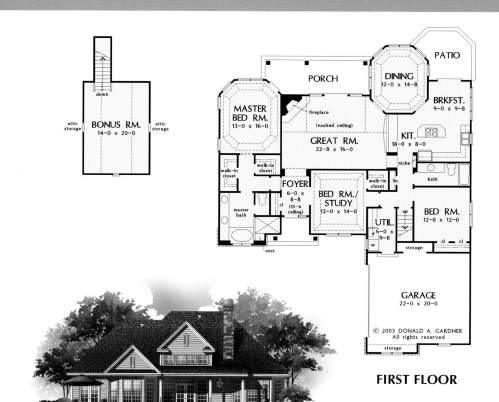

FIRST FLOOR

REAR ELEVATION

Plan AHBDG01-1013

- Total Living: 1929 s.f.
- Bonus Room: 335 s.f.
- 3 Bedrooms, 2 Baths
- Width: 54'8"
- Depth: 68'4"
- Crawlspace Foundation
- Price Category C

1-800-388-7580
www.affordablehomesforeverystageoflife.com

Donald A. Gardner Architects, Inc.

Transitions
Donald A. Gardner Architects, Inc.

We packed our luggage, cleaned the house and gave the neighbor a key in case of emergency. Three weeks into our drive across the country, I became homesick, but we did it.

© 2003 Donald A. Gardner, Inc.

The Iverson

Plan AHBDG01-1023

- Total Living: 1547 s.f.
- Bonus Room: 391 s.f.
- 3 Bedrooms, 2 Baths
- Width: 51'8"
- Depth: 59'0"
- Crawlspace Foundation
- Price Category C

1-800-388-7580
www.affordablehomesforeverystageoflife.com

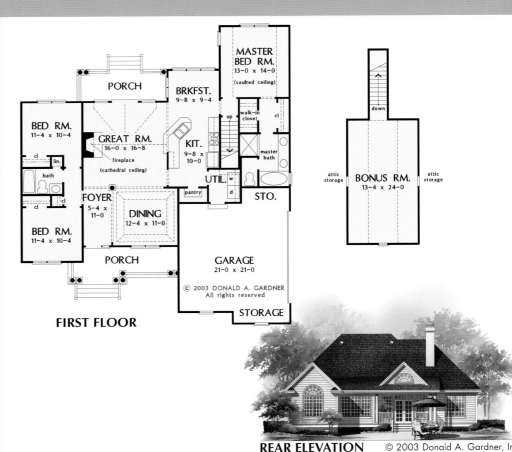

FIRST FLOOR

REAR ELEVATION   © 2003 Donald A. Gardner, Inc.

O ur twins went to a theme park for the first time. When we got back home, they talked about the rollercoasters until they fell asleep on the sofa.

The Holcombe

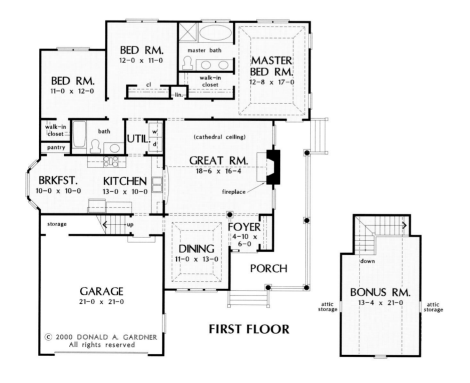

FIRST FLOOR

Plan AHBDG01-900

- Total Living: 1687 s.f.
- Bonus Room: 333 s.f.
- 3 Bedrooms, 2 Baths
- Width: 48'8"
- Depth: 59'4"
- Crawlspace Foundation
- Price Category C

1-800-388-7580
www.affordablehomesforeverystageoflife.com

Donald A. Gardner Architects, Inc.

Shortly after I accepted my job transfer, my company informed me of a neighborhood full of charming, new houses. I moved into this home, and everything's worked out great.

© 2002 Donald A. Gardner, Inc.

The Bakersfield

Plan AHBDG01-965

- Total Living: 1711 s.f.
- Bonus Room: 328 s.f.
- 3 Bedrooms, 2 Baths
- Width: 46'6"
- Depth: 65'0"
- Crawlspace Foundation
- Price Category C

1-800-388-7580
www.affordablehomesforeverystageoflife.com

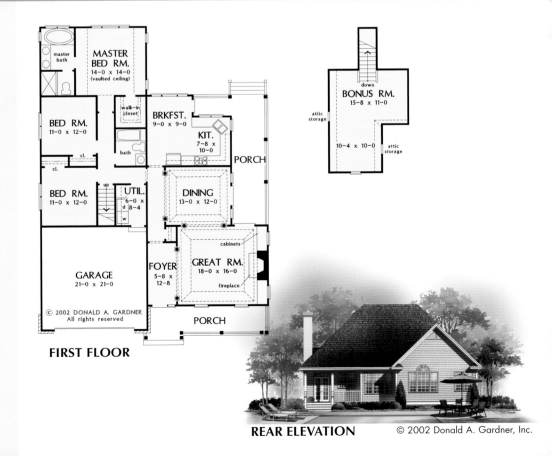

FIRST FLOOR

REAR ELEVATION   © 2002 Donald A. Gardner, Inc.

t was our child's history project that spurred our interest in discovering our ancestors. Our breakfast nook houses a table and desk and has become the hub for conducting research.

The Yarrow

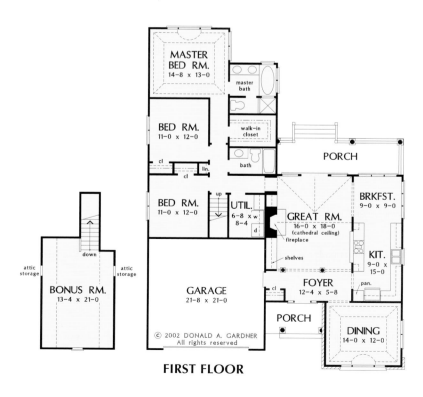

MASTER BED RM.
14-8 x 13-0

master bath

BED RM.
11-0 x 12-0

walk-in closet

bath

PORCH

cl lin.

BED RM.
11-0 x 12-0

UTIL.
6-8 x w
8-4

up

BRKFST.
9-0 x 9-0

GREAT RM.
16-0 x 18-0
(cathedral ceiling)
fireplace

KIT.
9-0 x 15-0

shelves

attic storage

attic storage

down

BONUS RM.
13-4 x 21-0

GARAGE
21-8 x 21-0

cl

FOYER
12-4 x 5-8

pan.

PORCH

DINING
14-0 x 12-0

FIRST FLOOR

Plan AHBDG01-988

- Total Living: 1707 s.f.
- Bonus Room: 323 s.f.
- 3 Bedrooms, 2 Baths
- Width: 48'6"
- Depth: 65'6"
- Crawlspace Foundation
- Price Category C

1-800-388-7580
www.affordablehomesforeverystageoflife.com

Donald A. Gardner Architects, Inc.

After my husband's operation, he was pretty much confined to the master suite. As he regained his strength, he would journey to the porch and kitchen, which were close by.

The Crabtree

Plan AHBDG01-817

- Total Living: 1828 s.f.
- Bonus Room: 352 s.f.
- 3 Bedrooms, 2 Baths
- Width: 53'8"
- Depth: 55'8"
- Crawlspace Foundation
- Price Category C

1-800-388-7580
www.affordablehomesforeverystageoflife.com

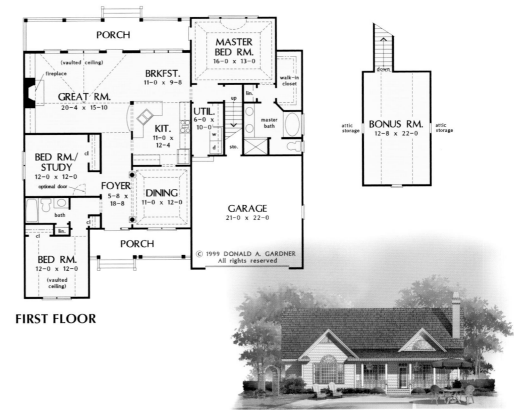

FIRST FLOOR

REAR ELEVATION

This home was more than a major purchase; it's the biggest investment we've ever made. We love it, and we have plenty of room to meet future needs.

The Saluda

FIRST FLOOR

SECOND FLOOR

REAR ELEVATION

Plan AHBDG01-795

- Total Living: 1891 s.f.
- First Floor: 1309 s.f.
- Second Floor: 582 s.f.
- Bonus Room: 570 s.f.
- 3 Bedrooms, 2-1/2 Baths
- Width: 65'8"
- Depth: 39'4"
- Crawlspace Foundation
- Price Category C

1-800-388-7580
www.affordablehomesforeverystageoflife.com

Donald A. Gardner Architects, Inc.

I was in the great room when my husband entered the foyer with a dozen roses. He informed me that I would be having dinner with a board member — him.

The Marigold

Plan AHBDG01-880

- Total Living: 1968 s.f.
- First Floor: 1437 s.f.
- Second Floor: 531 s.f.
- 3 Bedrooms, 2-1/2 Baths
- Width: 51'4"
- Depth: 41'6"
- Crawlspace Foundation
- Price Category C

1-800-388-7580
www.affordablehomesforeverystageoflife.com

FIRST FLOOR

SECOND FLOOR

REAR ELEVATION

O ne Saturday a month is devoted to volunteering. The whole family gets up early, meets in the kitchen and enjoys a hearty breakfast before we head out together.

The Fieldstone

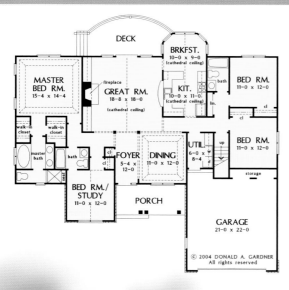

FIRST FLOOR

Plan AHBDG01-1047

- Total Living: 1975 s.f.
- Bonus Room: 361 s.f.
- 4 Bedrooms, 3 Baths
- Width: 62'0"
- Depth: 57'8"
- Crawlspace Foundation
- Price Category C

1-800-388-7580
www.affordablehomesforeverystageoflife.com

REAR ELEVATION   © 2004 Donald A. Gardner, Inc.

Donald A. Gardner Architects, Inc.

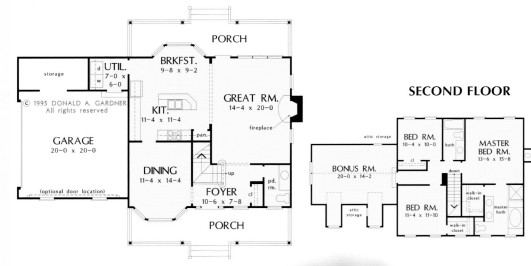

Transitions
Donald A. Gardner Architects, Inc.

We spent months preparing a room for our eight-year-old, and now that he's here, we feel that adopting him has made our home and lives complete.

© 1995 Donald A. Gardner Architects, Inc.

The Reidville

Plan AHBDG01-424

- Total Living: 1792 s.f.
- First Floor: 959 s.f.
- Second Floor: 833 s.f.
- Bonus Room: 344 s.f.
- 3 Bedrooms, 2-1/2 Baths
- Width: 52'6"
- Depth: 42'8"
- Crawlspace Foundation
- Price Category C

1-800-388-7580
www.affordablehomesforeverystageoflife.com

Affordable Homes

FIRST FLOOR

SECOND FLOOR

storage

UTIL.
7-0 x
6-0

BRKFST.
9-8 x 9-2

PORCH

© 1995 DONALD A. GARDNER
All rights reserved

KIT.
11-4 x 11-4

GREAT RM.
14-4 x 20-0

fireplace

GARAGE
20-0 x 20-0

pan.

DINING
11-4 x 14-4

up

FOYER
10-6 x 7-8

pd.
rm.

(optional door location)

PORCH

attic storage

BED RM.
10-4 x 10-0

bath

**MASTER
BED RM.**
13-6 x 15-8

cl

BONUS RM.
20-0 x 14-2

down

walk-in
closet

attic
storage

BED RM.
11-4 x 11-10

walk-in
closet

master
bath

REAR ELEVATION   © 1995 Donald A. Gardner Architects, Inc.

We recently purchased our first stocks. We spent many weeks researching, and now it's becoming my husband's hobby. He ran down from the bonus room to tell me about the money we made.

The Griffin

REAR ELEVATION © 1997 Donald A. Gardner Architects, Inc.

BONUS RM.
12-8 x 18-4
attic storage   attic storage
skylight
down

DECK

master bath
(cathedral ceiling)
fireplace   DINING
12-0 x 12-0
GREAT RM.
15-0 x 17-10
lin.
walk-in closet
bath   lin.
BED RM.
11-0 x 11-0

MASTER BED RM.
13-0 x 15-0
KIT.
12-0 x 12-2
UTIL.
6-4 x 6-0   w d   cl
BED RM.
11-0 x 11-0

walk-in closet   FOYER
6-2 x 6-0   cl
up   storage

PORCH

© 1997 DONALD A. GARDNER
All rights reserved

GARAGE
20-0 x 20-4

FIRST FLOOR

Plan AHBDG01-535

- Total Living: 1517 s.f.
- Bonus Room: 287 s.f.
- 3 Bedrooms, 2 Baths
- Width: 61'4"
- Depth: 48'6"
- Crawlspace Foundation
- Price Category C

1-800-388-7580
www.affordablehomesforeverystageoflife.com

Donald A. Gardner Architects, Inc.

y Mom switched careers. She currently teaches at my school and knows all my teachers. Now when I get home from school, I go straight to my room and do my homework.

The Schuyler

Plan AHBDG01-766

- Total Living: 1559 s.f.
- 3 Bedrooms, 2 Baths
- Width: 54'4"
- Depth: 52'0"
- Crawlspace Foundation
- Price Category C

1-800-388-7580
www.affordablehomesforeverystageoflife.com

FIRST FLOOR

REAR ELEVATION

must have a row full of my favorite author's books in our study, and it was an absolute privilege to meet her and have her autograph her new book for me.

Donald A. Gardner Architects, Inc.

© 1993 Donald A. Gardner Architects, Inc.

The Tremont

SECOND FLOOR

LOFT/ STUDY
10–4 x 14–0

master bath

walk-in closet

railing

down

(cathedral ceiling)
great room below

MASTER BED RM.
11–8 x 15–8

attic storage

clerestory windows

FIRST FLOOR

PORCH
33–10 x 6–4

DINING
12–0 x 12–2

KIT.
9–4 x 12–2

cl
cl

BED RM.
11–8 x 12–8

balcony above

bath
w
d

cl

GREAT RM.
17–4 x 16–6

fireplace

up

© 1993 DONALD A. GARDNER
All rights reserved

BED RM./ STUDY
11–8 x 14–0

cl

PORCH
21–6 x 6–4

Plan AHBDG01-301

- Total Living: 1713 s.f.
- First Floor: 1146 s.f.
- Second Floor: 567 s.f.
- 3 Bedrooms, 2 Baths
- Width: 36'5"
- Depth: 43'8"
- Crawlspace Foundation
- Price Category C

1-800-388-7580
www.affordablehomesforeverystageoflife.com

REAR ELEVATION   © 1993 Donald A. Gardner Architects, Inc.

Donald A. Gardner Architects, Inc.

I remember the first time I saw the ocean; it was so overwhelming. I had always wanted a house at the beach, and this one is perfect for the Lowcountry.

The Williamston

Plan AHBDG01-391

- Total Living: 1991 s.f.
- First Floor: 1480 s.f.
- Second Floor: 511 s.f.
- Bonus Room: 363 s.f.
- 3 Bedrooms, 2-1/2 Baths
- Width: 73'0"
- Depth: 45'0"
- Crawlspace Foundation
- Price Category C

1-800-388-7580
www.affordablehomesforeverystageoflife.com

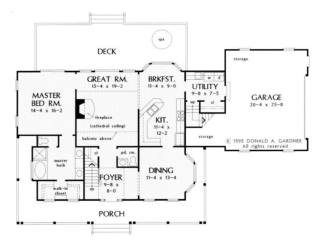

FIRST FLOOR

DECK
spa
GREAT RM. 15-4 x 19-2
BRKFST. 11-4 9-0
storage
UTILITY 9-8 x 7-5
GARAGE 20-4 x 25-8
MASTER BED RM. 14-4 x 16-2
fireplace
(cathedral ceiling)
balcony above
KIT. 11-4 x 12-2
storage
cl
master bath
pd. rm.
DINING 11-4 x 13-4
FOYER 9-8 x 8-0
walk-in closet
up
PORCH

SECOND FLOOR

skylights
BONUS RM. 12-8 x 25-8
attic storage
down
attic storage
great room below
attic storage
attic storage
railing
BED RM. 11-4 x 12-6
down
bath
BED RM. 11-4 x 12-6
cl
cl
foyer below

REAR ELEVATION

When my mother-in-law came to live with us, we converted the bonus room into our son's room, and moved Mom in his room next to the kitchen.

The Brisbane

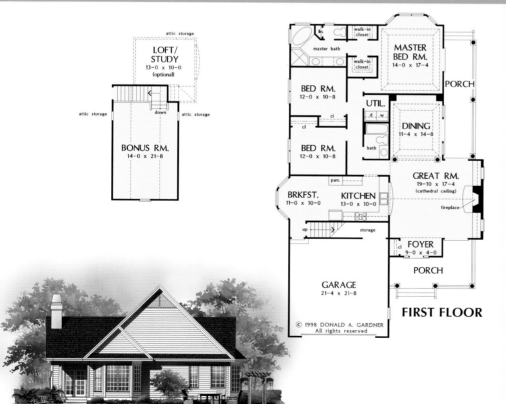

LOFT/ STUDY
13-0 x 10-0
(optional)

attic storage   down   attic storage

BONUS RM.
14-0 x 21-8

MASTER BED RM.
14-0 x 17-4

master bath   walk-in closet   walk-in closet

BED RM.
12-0 x 10-8

UTIL.
d | w   bath

DINING
11-4 x 14-8

BED RM.
12-0 x 10-8

PORCH

pan.

GREAT RM.
19-10 x 17-4
(cathedral ceiling)

fireplace

BRKFST.
11-0 x 10-0

KITCHEN
13-0 x 10-0

up   storage

FOYER
9-0 x 4-0

cl

GARAGE
21-4 x 21-8

PORCH

FIRST FLOOR

Plan AHBDG01-705

- Total Living: 1795 s.f.
- Bonus Room: 368 s.f.
- 3 Bedrooms, 2 Baths
- Width: 45'0"
- Depth: 72'4"
- Crawlspace Foundation
- Price Category C

1-800-388-7580
www.affordablehomesforeverystageoflife.com

REAR ELEVATION

Donald A. Gardner Architects, Inc.

89

Welcoming everything from first dates to new careers, the affordable homes in this section demonstrate how having a step-saving design increases easy living. By using columns in place of walls, cut-throughs decrease the number of steps it takes to reach certain destinations. Positioning also plays a large part, especially in the kitchens, reducing the amount of steps it takes to complete tasks and chores.

Turning Points

ents when important changes occur

Ranch-like WELCOME

(Left) Buttery walls, a vaulted ceiling and fireplace create a sophisticated great room.

(Right) Country and Traditional styles combine to form a brick home with gables and a wide front porch.

(Below) Decorative molding and trim add a subtle elegance to this formal dining room.

© 1997 Donald A. Gardner Architects, Inc.

The Cloverdale

"It was quite an adjustment — going back to school after all these years. My kids ask me if I want to come to their rooms and do my homework, but the morning table in the breakfast nook is my favorite place to study. And occasionally, the kids make me snacks when I'm studying for a big exam."

Turning Points
Donald A. Gardner Architects, Inc.

(Left) The great room opens into the kitchen, so cooking and conversation can happen simultaneously.

(Below) The bright breakfast nook is extended by a beautiful bay window.

(Right) Honey-stained cabinetry and a tiled backsplash combine to create a cozy kitchen.

This home combines the Victorian charm of yesteryear with a plan designed for today's families. Accented by columns, the great room with fireplace is vaulted, while the foyer, dining room, kitchen, breakfast bay and bedroom/study boast impressive ten-foot ceilings. With double-door entry, the secluded master suite features a tray ceiling, walk-in closet and private, skylit bath.

Affordable Homes • The Designs of Donald A. Gardner Architects, Inc.

The Cloverdale

1-800-388-7580

www.afforadablehomesforeverystageoflife.com

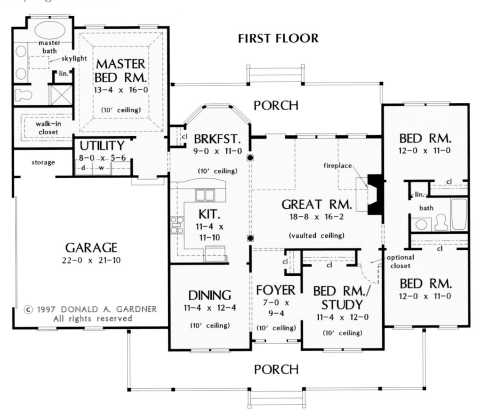

FIRST FLOOR

master bath

skylight

lin.

MASTER BED RM.
13-4 x 16-0

(10' ceiling)

walk-in closet

storage

UTILITY
8-0 x 5-6
d — w

GARAGE
22-0 x 21-10

cl

BRKFST.
9-0 x 11-0

(10' ceiling)

KIT.
11-4 x 11-10

DINING
11-4 x 12-4

(10' ceiling)

PORCH

GREAT RM.
18-8 x 16-2

(vaulted ceiling)

fireplace

cl

cl

FOYER
7-0 x 9-4

(10' ceiling)

BED RM./ STUDY
11-4 x 12-0

(10' ceiling)

PORCH

BED RM.
12-0 x 11-0

cl

lin.

bath

optional closet

cl

BED RM.
12-0 x 11-0

Three additional bedrooms are located on the opposite side of the house and share a full bath with linen closet. Front and back porches extend the living space to the outdoors, and the two-car garage offers ample storage space.

(Far Left) Low-maintenance brick helps families spend more time on recreation instead of upkeep.
(Left) The study can transform into a secondary bedroom as needs change.
(Below Left) Modified from the original plan, the rear porch was screened to increase fresh-air enjoyment.
(Below) A tray ceiling visually lifts the look of the master bedroom, expanding volume.

Plan AHBDG01-490

- Total Living: 1903 s.f.
- 4 Bedrooms, 2 Baths
- Width: 65'8"
- Depth: 55'7"
- Crawlspace Foundation
- Price Category C

Photographed home may have been modified from the original construction documents.

"Deciding to stay at home with the children after they were born wasn't a hard choice to make. We discussed it before we decided to have children, and that was part of the reason we chose this house. It had the square footage and growing room we required; plus it had the architectural details and floorplan we wanted."

The Altamont

1-800-388-7580

www.afforadablehomesforeverystageoflife.com

Plan AHBDG01-377

- Total Living: 1787 s.f.
- Bonus Room: 326 s.f.
- 3 Bedrooms, 2 Baths
- Width: 66'2"
- Depth: 66'8"
- Crawlspace Foundation
- Price Category C

Photographed home may have been modified from the original construction documents.

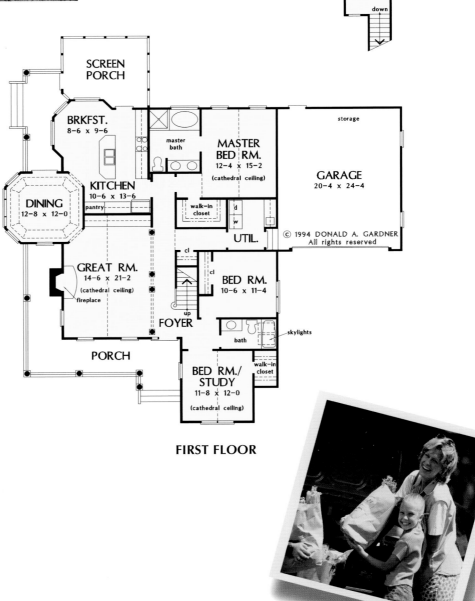

BONUS RM.
14-2 x 17-10

down

SCREEN PORCH

BRKFST.
8-6 x 9-6

master bath

MASTER BED RM.
12-4 x 15-2
(cathedral ceiling)

storage

GARAGE
20-4 x 24-4

DINING
12-8 x 12-0

KITCHEN
10-6 x 13-6

pantry

walk-in closet

UTIL.

GREAT RM.
14-6 x 21-2
(cathedral ceiling)
fireplace

cl

cl

BED RM.
10-6 x 11-4

up

FOYER

bath

skylights

PORCH

BED RM./ STUDY
11-8 x 12-0
(cathedral ceiling)

walk-in closet

FIRST FLOOR

Turning Points
Donald A. Gardner Architects, Inc.

StylishSpaces

(Left) A fireplace, built-in cabinets and French doors highlight this great room.

(Right) Light cabinetry and granite countertops showcase stainless steel appliances.

(Below) A transom and tray ceiling add subtle formality to this dining room.

The Kilpatrick

"Starting a new hobby introduces change. My hobby started my second career. I have always been passionate about photography, and now that I've taken a few classes, I've turned my bonus room into a darkroom and home studio. When clients enter the foyer, they have easy access to my studio upstairs."

The Kilpatrick

1-800-388-7580

www.afforadablehomesforeverystageoflife.com

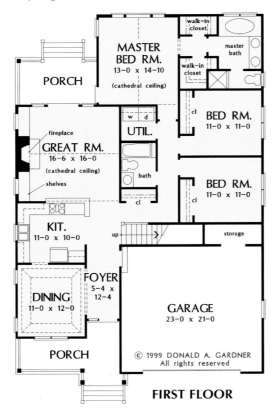

MASTER BED RM.
13-0 x 14-10
(cathedral ceiling)

PORCH

walk-in closet

master bath

walk-in closet

fireplace

GREAT RM.
16-6 x 16-0
(cathedral ceiling)

shelves

w d

UTIL.

bath

cl

BED RM.
11-0 x 11-0

cl

cl

BED RM.
11-0 x 11-0

cl

KIT.
11-0 x 10-0

up

storage

FOYER
5-4 x 12-4

DINING
11-0 x 12-0

GARAGE
23-0 x 21-0

PORCH

FIRST FLOOR

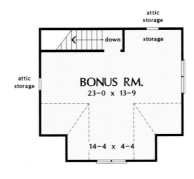

attic storage

down

storage

attic storage

BONUS RM.
23-0 x 13-9

14-4 x 4-4

Affordable Homes • The Designs of Donald A. Gardner Architects, Inc.

A tray ceiling tops the dining room, while the kitchen features an efficient design and is open to the great room with cathedral ceiling, fireplace and built-ins. A nearby staircase leads to a generous bonus room, and the master suite enjoys a cathedral ceiling, back porch access, dual walk-ins and a well-appointed bath.

(**Far Left**) Decorative brackets add a cottage ambiance to this narrow-lot home.
(**Left**) Brick fashions a beautiful porch floor, adding architectural interest.
(**Below**) With a vaulted ceiling and built-ins, this bonus room makes a great retreat.

Plan AHBDG01-833

- Total Living: 1608 s.f.
- Bonus Room: 437 s.f.
- 3 Bedrooms, 2 Baths
- Width: 40'8"
- Depth: 62'8"
- Crawlspace Foundation
- Price Category C

Photographed home may have been modified from the original construction documents.

Country Revisited

(Left) This porch and its wicker rockers encourage outdoor relaxation.

(Right) A spectacular Palladian window ushers light into the two-story foyer.

(Below) The kitchen opens to the breakfast nook, so parents can cook and help with afternoon homework.

© 1991 Donald A. Gardner Architects, Inc.

The Merrifield

" We started a new diet and exercise routine in order to establish a healthier lifestyle. In the mornings, we usually work up an appetite in the gym and head downstairs for a smoothie to start the day off right. The layout of our kitchen allows us to cook dinner together, so we get to spend time with each other while preparing healthy meals. "

The Merrifield

1-800-388-7580

www.afforadablehomesforeverystageoflife.com

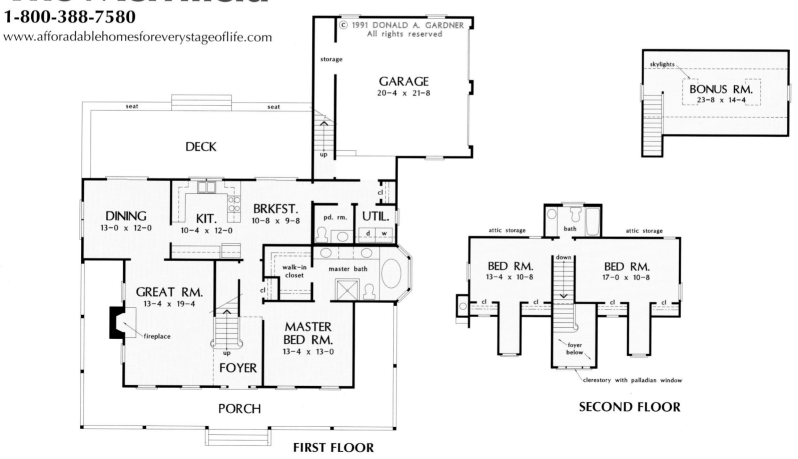

storage

GARAGE
20-4 x 21-8

skylights

BONUS RM.
23-8 x 14-4

seat   seat

DECK

DINING
13-0 x 12-0

KIT.
10-4 x 12-0

BRKFST.
10-8 x 9-8

pd. rm.

UTIL.
d w

cl

walk-in closet

master bath

cl

GREAT RM.
13-4 x 19-4

fireplace

up

FOYER

MASTER BED RM.
13-4 x 13-0

PORCH

FIRST FLOOR

attic storage   bath   attic storage

BED RM.
13-4 x 10-8

down

BED RM.
17-0 x 10-8

cl   cl   cl   cl

foyer below

clerestory with palladian window

SECOND FLOOR

Affordable Homes • The Designs of Donald A. Gardner Architects, Inc.

Turning Points
Donald A. Gardner Architects, Inc.

A luxurious wraparound porch, voluminous ceilings and the two-story foyer illuminated by a clerestory dormer with Palladian window create casual elegance. The master suite includes a private bath with a double vanity, separate shower and garden tub, while upstairs, secondary bedrooms share a full bath. A versatile bonus room and a basement plan provide room for growth.

(Far Left) With stately columns and a deep, overhanging front porch, this home complements any streetscape.
(Left) French doors lead from the dining room to the rear deck, promoting alfresco dining.
(Below) The great room demonstrates this home's incredible traffic flow.

Plan AHBDG01-235

- Total Living: 1898 s.f.
- First Floor: 1356 s.f.
- Second Floor: 542 s.f.
- Bonus Room: 393 s.f.
- 3 Bedrooms, 2-1/2 Baths
- Width: 59'0"
- Depth: 64'4"
- Crawlspace Foundation
- Price Category C

"We knew the day would come when our last child would move out, but it wasn't until after both children finished college and moved into apartments that we transformed their rooms into a guest bedroom and study. We didn't know if they would come back or not. It's funny, but we've gotten used to having the house to ourselves."

The Georgetown

1-800-388-7580
www.afforadablehomesforeverystageoflife.com

Plan AHBDG01-393

- Total Living: 1832 s.f.
- Bonus Room: 425 s.f.
- 3 Bedrooms, 2 Baths
- Width: 65'4"
- Depth: 62'0"
- Crawlspace Foundation
- Price Category C

Photographed home may have been modified from the original construction documents.

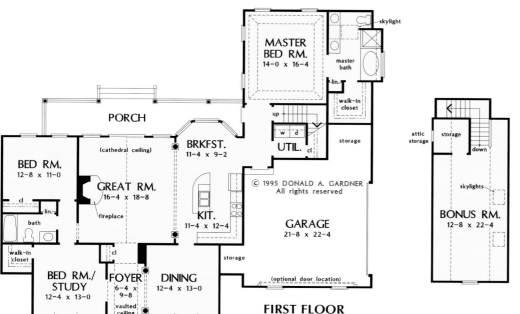

FIRST FLOOR

MASTER BED RM. 14-0 x 16-4
master bath
skylight
walk-in closet
PORCH
BRKFST. 11-4 x 9-2
UTIL.
up
w d
storage
BED RM. 12-8 x 11-0
(cathedral ceiling)
GREAT RM. 16-4 x 18-8
fireplace
KIT. 11-4 x 12-4
© 1995 DONALD A. GARDNER All rights reserved
GARAGE 21-8 x 22-4
walk-in closet
bath
lin.
cl
BED RM./ STUDY 12-4 x 13-0
FOYER 6-4 x 9-8
vaulted ceiling
DINING 12-4 x 13-0
storage
(optional door location)
PORCH

BONUS RM. 12-8 x 22-4
attic storage
storage
down
skylights

My wife and I were in the great room watching television when my daughter ran inside, saying "Look. Look." It was her first paycheck. I remembered how exciting my first check was.

© 2002 Donald A. Gardner, Inc.

The Luxembourg

Plan AHBDG01-979

- Total Living: 1797 s.f.
- First Floor: 1345 s.f.
- Second Floor: 452 s.f.
- Bonus Room: 349 s.f.
- 3 Bedrooms, 2-1/2 Baths
- Width: 63'0"
- Depth: 40'0"
- Crawlspace Foundation
- Price Category C

1-800-388-7580
www.affordablehomesforeverystageoflife.com

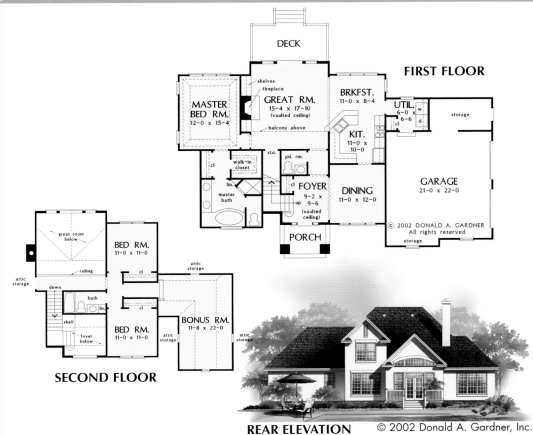

DECK

FIRST FLOOR

MASTER BED RM.
12-0 x 15-4

GREAT RM.
15-4 x 17-10
(vaulted ceiling)

shelves fireplace
balcony above

BRKFST.
11-0 x 8-4

UTIL.
6-0 x 6-6

storage

KIT.
11-0 x 10-0

walk-in closet

master bath

FOYER
9-2 x 9-6
(vaulted ceiling)

DINING
11-0 x 12-0

GARAGE
21-0 x 22-0

PORCH

© 2002 DONALD A. GARDNER
All rights reserved

storage

great room below

railing

attic storage

down

BED RM.
11-0 x 11-0

attic storage

bath

shelf

foyer below

BED RM.
11-0 x 11-0

BONUS RM.
11-8 x 22-0

attic storage

SECOND FLOOR

REAR ELEVATION © 2002 Donald A. Gardner, Inc.

J oining the Peace Corps was a life-changing experience. I enjoyed my tropical assignment, and when I got back to the States and was looking for a home, a screened porch was a must-have.

The Joliet

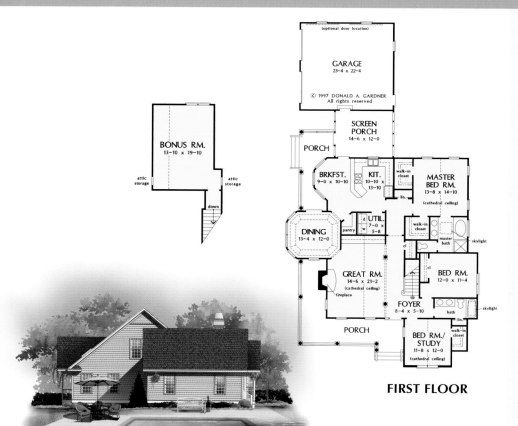

REAR ELEVATION

FIRST FLOOR

Plan AHBDG01-504

- Total Living: 1918 s.f.
- Bonus Room: 307 s.f.
- 3 Bedrooms, 2 Baths
- Width: 48'8"
- Depth: 89'6"
- Crawlspace Foundation
- Price Category C

1-800-388-7580
www.affordablehomesforeverystageoflife.com

Donald A. Gardner Architects, Inc.

My husband said a year-old argument shouldn't come between him and his brother, so he called him. When I got home from work, they were on the deck, laughing.

© 1999 Donald A. Gardner, Inc.

The Truesdale

Plan AHBDG01-813

- Total Living: 1650 s.f.
- Bonus Room: 394 s.f.
- 3 Bedrooms, 2 Baths
- Width: 56'8"
- Depth: 49'7"
- Crawlspace Foundation
- Price Category C

1-800-388-7580
www.affordablehomesforeverystageoflife.com

FIRST FLOOR

REAR ELEVATION © 1999 Donald A. Gardner, Inc.

Somebody has to win the lottery, but I really never dreamed it would be us. Afterwards, we purchased some land in the country and built this house as a get-away.

The Chesden

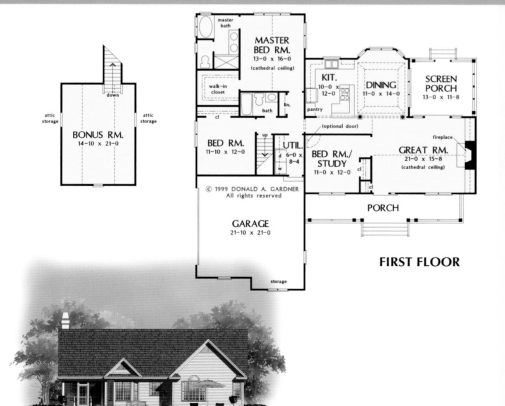

BONUS RM.
14-10 x 21-0

attic storage

down

master bath

MASTER BED RM.
13-0 x 16-0
(cathedral ceiling)

walk-in closet

bath

lin.

KIT.
10-0 x 12-0

pantry

DINING
11-0 x 14-0

SCREEN PORCH
13-0 x 11-8

BED RM.
11-10 x 12-0

up

UTIL.
d 6-0 x
w 8-4

BED RM./ STUDY
11-0 x 12-0

(optional door)

fireplace

GREAT RM.
21-0 x 15-8
(cathedral ceiling)

© 1999 DONALD A. GARDNER
All rights reserved

GARAGE
21-10 x 21-0

PORCH

storage

FIRST FLOOR

Plan AHBDG01-812

- Total Living: 1596 s.f.
- Bonus Room: 367 s.f.
- 3 Bedrooms, 2 Baths
- Width: 57'6"
- Depth: 58'2"
- Crawlspace Foundation
- Price Category C

1-800-388-7580
www.affordablehomesforeverystageoflife.com

Donald A. Gardner Architects, Inc.

113

REAR ELEVATION

At times our faith is tested and renewed within the comfort and security of our homes. In the quiet of certain rooms, I've had realizations or moments of enlightenment.

The Wilshire

Plan AHBDG01-976

- Total Living: 1904 s.f.
- Bonus Room: 366 s.f.
- 3 Bedrooms, 2 Baths
- Width: 53'10"
- Depth: 57'8"
- Crawlspace Foundation
- Price Category C

1-800-388-7580
www.affordablehomesforeverystageoflife.com

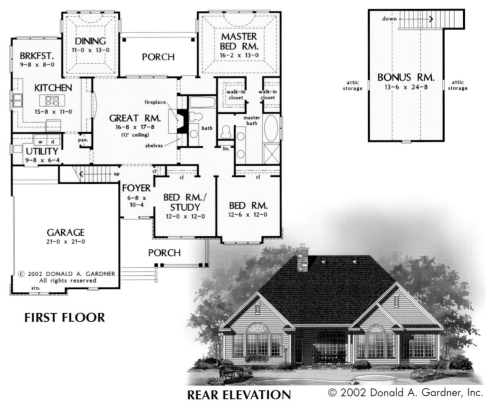

FIRST FLOOR

DINING 11-0 x 13-0
PORCH
MASTER BED RM. 16-2 x 13-0
BRKFST. 9-8 x 8-0
KITCHEN 15-8 x 11-0
walk-in closet
walk-in closet
fireplace
GREAT RM. 16-8 x 17-8 (12' ceiling)
master bath
bath
UTILITY 9-8 x 6-4
w d
pan.
shelves
lin.
FOYER 6-8 x 10-4
BED RM./STUDY 12-0 x 12-0
BED RM. 12-6 x 12-0
GARAGE 21-0 x 21-0
PORCH
cl
cl
cl
up

down
BONUS RM. 13-6 x 24-8
attic storage
attic storage

REAR ELEVATION

As a first-time father, the addition of step-children has been a life-changing experience. Upon their arrival, we decorated their bedrooms together, which provided an opportunity to bond.

The Carrington

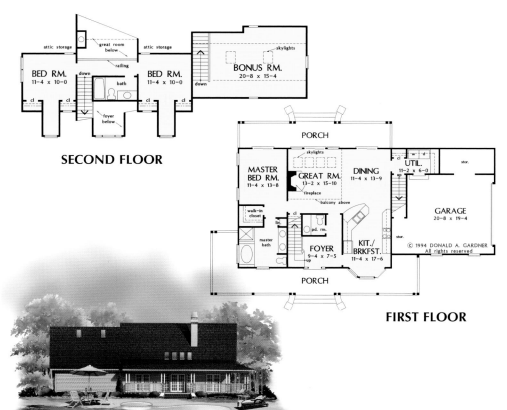

SECOND FLOOR

FIRST FLOOR

Plan AHBDG01-375

- Total Living: 1639 s.f.
- First Floor: 1180 s.f.
- Second Floor: 459 s.f.
- Bonus Room: 387 s.f.
- 3 Bedrooms, 2-1/2 Baths
- Width: 68'0"
- Depth: 42'7"
- Crawlspace Foundation
- Price Category C

1-800-388-7580
www.affordablehomesforeverystageoflife.com

Donald A. Gardner Architects, Inc.

REAR ELEVATION

We didn't expect to have children so soon — much less twins — but our house was designed to grow and change with our needs, which it has.

The Richfield

Plan AHBDG01-999

- Total Living: 1925 s.f.
- Bonus Room: 343 s.f.
- 3 Bedrooms, 2-1/2 Baths
- Width: 70'0"
- Depth: 49'8"
- Crawlspace Foundation
- Price Category C

1-800-388-7580
www.affordablehomesforeverystageoflife.com

My first "real" job afforded me the opportunity to put a down payment on my first house. I love this house, because it is newly constructed, yet possesses a timeless character.

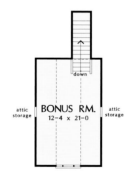

The Smythe

REAR ELEVATION © 2002 Donald A. Gardner, Inc.

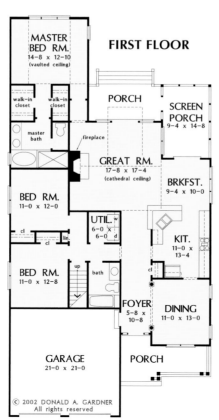

attic storage **BONUS RM.** 12-4 x 21-0 attic storage

down

MASTER BED RM. 14-8 x 12-10 (vaulted ceiling)

FIRST FLOOR

walk-in closet   walk-in closet

master bath

PORCH

SCREEN PORCH 9-4 x 14-8

fireplace

GREAT RM. 17-8 x 17-4 (cathedral ceiling)

BRKFST. 9-4 x 10-0

BED RM. 11-0 x 12-0

UTIL. 6-0 x 6-0

KIT. 11-0 x 13-4

cl   cl   lin.

BED RM. 11-0 x 12-8

up   bath

FOYER 5-8 x 10-8

DINING 11-0 x 13-0

GARAGE 21-0 x 21-0

PORCH

Plan AHBDG01-973

- Total Living: 1789 s.f.
- Bonus Room: 312 s.f.
- 3 Bedrooms, 2 Baths
- Width: 39'0"
- Depth: 79'4"
- Crawlspace Foundation
- Price Category C

1-800-388-7580
www.affordablehomesforeverystageoflife.com

Donald A. Gardner Architects, Inc.

When he decided to enlist in the military and postpone college, we were supportive of his decision. Now there are pictures of him in uniform throughout our home.

The Wilton

Plan AHBDG01-981

- Total Living: 1911 s.f.
- Bonus Room: 366 s.f.
- 3 Bedrooms, 2 Baths
- Width: 52'0"
- Depth: 69'10"
- Crawlspace Foundation
- Price Category C

1-800-388-7580
www.affordablehomesforeverystageoflife.com

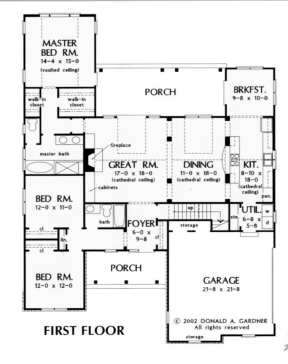

FIRST FLOOR

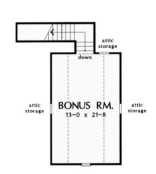

BONUS RM.
13-0 x 21-8

REAR ELEVATION   © 2002 Donald A. Gardner, Inc.

O ur granddaughter spends time with us when her parents are overseas. When we built this house, we gave her a room of her own — instead of her using a guestroom.

The Gillespie

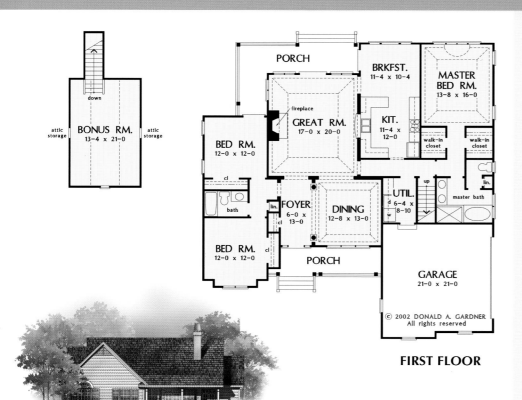

BONUS RM.
13-4 x 21-0
attic storage   attic storage
down

PORCH

BRKFST.
11-4 x 10-4

MASTER BED RM.
13-8 x 16-0

GREAT RM.
17-0 x 20-0
fireplace

KIT.
11-4 x 12-0

walk-in closet   walk-in closet

BED RM.
12-0 x 12-0
cl

BED RM.
12-0 x 12-0
cl

bath
lin.

FOYER
6-0 x 13-0
cl

DINING
12-8 x 13-0

UTIL.
6-4 x 8-10

master bath
lin.
up

PORCH

GARAGE
21-0 x 21-0

FIRST FLOOR

Plan AHBDG01-992

- Total Living: 1955 s.f.
- Bonus Room: 329 s.f.
- 3 Bedrooms, 2 Baths
- Width: 56'0"
- Depth: 58'4"
- Crawlspace Foundation
- Price Category C

1-800-388-7580
www.affordablehomesforeverystageoflife.com

REAR ELEVATION

Donald A. Gardner Architects, Inc.

We've been getting ready for our first joint art showing. We have canvases lined up against every wall in the great room to help us choose the ones we want to show.

The Upton

Plan AHBDG01-938

- Total Living: 1929 s.f.
- 3 Bedrooms, 2 Baths
- Width: 46'11"
- Depth: 71'11"
- Crawlspace Foundation
- Price Category C

1-800-388-7580
www.affordablehomesforeverystageoflife.com

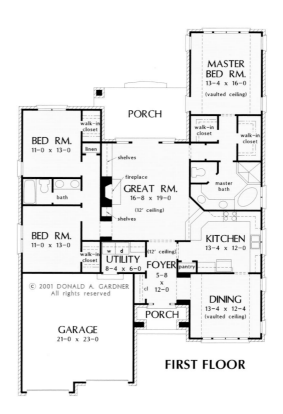

FIRST FLOOR

MASTER BED RM.
13-4 x 16-0
(vaulted ceiling)

PORCH

BED RM.
11-0 x 13-0

walk-in closet

linen

shelves

fireplace

walk-in closet

walk-in closet

bath

GREAT RM.
16-8 x 19-0
(12' ceiling)

master bath

shelves

BED RM.
11-0 x 13-0

KITCHEN
13-4 x 12-0

walk-in closet

w   d

UTILITY
8-4 x 6-0

(12' ceiling)

FOYER
5-8 x 12-0

pantry

cl

DINING
13-4 x 12-4
(vaulted ceiling)

GARAGE
21-0 x 23-0

PORCH

I

was putting away laundry when he told me he had something important to tell me. We sat on the edge of the bed — he said he found his birth parents.

© 1998 Donald A. Gardner, Inc.

The Courtney

SECOND FLOOR

FIRST FLOOR

REAR ELEVATION   © 1998 Donald A. Gardner, Inc.

Plan AHBDG01-706

- Total Living: 1859 s.f.
- First Floor: 1336 s.f.
- Second Floor: 523 s.f.
- Bonus Room: 225 s.f.
- 3 Bedrooms, 2-1/2 Baths
- Width: 45'0"
- Depth: 53'0"
- Crawlspace Foundation
- Price Category C

1-800-388-7580
www.affordablehomesforeverystageoflife.com

Donald A. Gardner Architects, Inc.   **121**

I'm finally able to work from home after spending years in a corporate setting. The bonus room provides the perfect home office and even has a service entrance.

The Windemere

Plan AHBDG01-760

- Total Living: 1511 s.f.
- Bonus Room: 549 s.f.
- 3 Bedrooms, 2 Baths
- Width: 71'4"
- Depth: 45'0"
- Crawlspace Foundation
- Price Category C

1-800-388-7580
www.affordablehomesforeverystageoflife.com

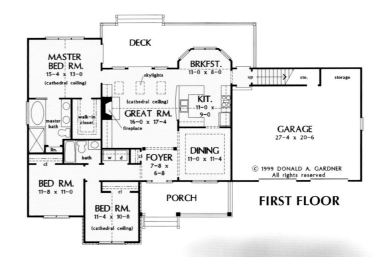

FIRST FLOOR

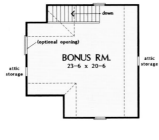

BONUS RM.
23-6 x 20-6

REAR ELEVATION

Every year — without fail — my best friend sends me a flower arrangement to mark the day I saved her life. They arrived today and look beautiful on my breakfast counter.

The Applemoor

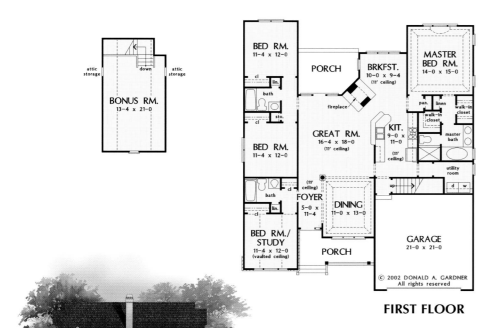

FIRST FLOOR

REAR ELEVATION © 2002 Donald A. Gardner, Inc.

Plan AHBDG01-970

- Total Living: 1952 s.f.
- Bonus Room: 339 s.f.
- 4 Bedrooms, 3 Baths
- Width: 50'0"
- Depth: 60'0"
- Crawlspace Foundation
- Price Category C

1-800-388-7580
www.affordablehomesforeverystageoflife.com

Donald A. Gardner Architects, Inc.

123

When I received my inheritance, we built this house and moved out of that cramped apartment. We love the open floorplan and room to grow. We just bought a puppy.

The Creston

Plan AHBDG01-420

- Total Living: 1972 s.f.
- First Floor: 1436 s.f.
- Second Floor: 536 s.f.
- Bonus Room: 296 s.f.
- 3 Bedrooms, 2-1/2 Baths
- Width: 67'10"
- Depth: 47'4"
- Crawlspace Foundation
- Price Category C

1-800-388-7580
www.affordablehomesforeverystageoflife.com

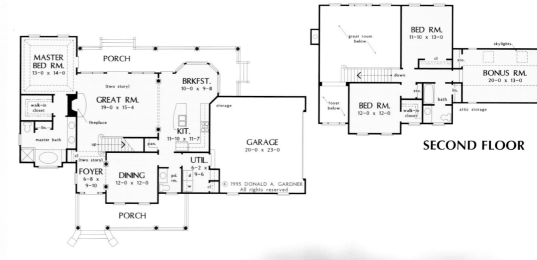

FIRST FLOOR

SECOND FLOOR

REAR ELEVATION © 1995 Donald A. Gardner Architects, Inc.

I

t seems that every television in the house has been on around the clock, but what we noticed is the amount of patriotism surfacing in the community.

The Callison

SECOND FLOOR

FIRST FLOOR

Plan AHBDG01-411

- Total Living: 1846 s.f.
- First Floor: 1380 s.f.
- Second Floor: 466 s.f.
- Bonus Room: 326 s.f.
- 3 Bedrooms, 2-1/2 Baths
- Width: 61'8"
- Depth: 65'0"
- Crawlspace Foundation
- Price Category C

1-800-388-7580
www.affordablehomesforeverystageoflife.com

Donald A. Gardner Architects, Inc.

125

REAR ELEVATION © 1995 Donald A. Gardner Architects, Inc.

He rang the doorbell, and my husband answered the door. They talked in the great room until she was ready. This was her official "first date."

The Mayfield

Plan AHBDG01-537

- Total Living: 1899 s.f.
- Bonus Room: 315 s.f.
- 3 Bedrooms, 2 Baths
- Width: 58'8"
- Depth: 66'10"
- Crawlspace Foundation
- Price Category C

1-800-388-7580
www.affordablehomesforeverystageoflife.com

FIRST FLOOR

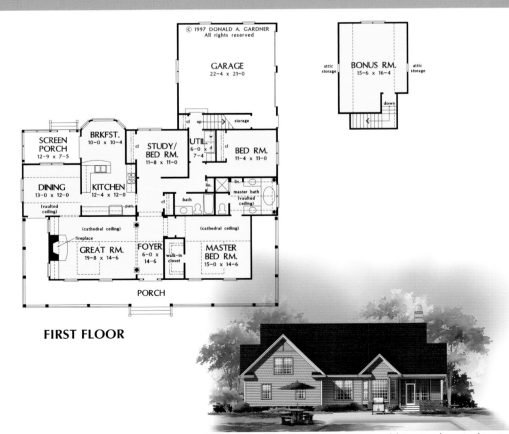

REAR ELEVATION © 1997 Donald A. Gardner Architects, In

We hung tennis balls from the garage ceiling to assist him with parking. My wife was a little teary about his driver's permit; it seems that he was a toddler just yesterday.

The Woodsfield

FIRST FLOOR

REAR ELEVATION © 1994 Donald A. Gardner Architects, Inc.

Plan AHBDG01-341

- Total Living: 1954 s.f.
- Bonus Room: 436 s.f.
- 3 Bedrooms, 2-1/2 Baths
- Width: 71'11"
- Depth: 57'3"
- Crawlspace Foundation
- Price Category C

1-800-388-7580
www.affordablehomesforeverystageoflife.com

Donald A. Gardner Architects, Inc.

I have always loved baking, but I was afraid to pursue it as a career. I found the courage with the support of my family and started my business in my own kitchen.

© 1999 Donald A. Gardner, Inc.

The Whitaker

Plan AHBDG01-835

- Total Living: 1671 s.f.
- Bonus Room: 348 s.f.
- 3 Bedrooms, 2 Baths
- Width: 50'8"
- Depth: 52'4"
- Crawlspace Foundation
- Price Category C

1-800-388-7580
www.affordablehomesforeverystageoflife.com

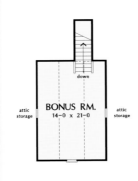

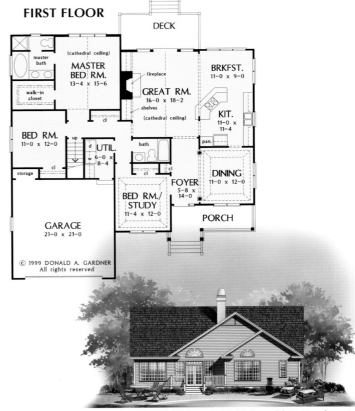

FIRST FLOOR

© 1999 DONALD A. GARDNER
All rights reserved

REAR ELEVATION © 1999 Donald A. Gardner, Inc.

I was sitting on the deck when I realized how quickly the last ten years had passed. I took pictures to the dining room table and began organizing albums.

The Somerset

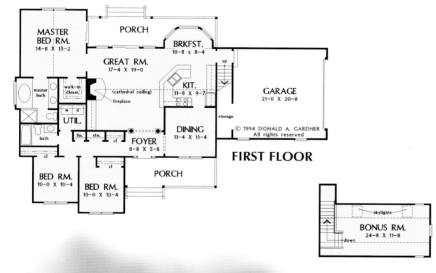

Plan AHBDG01-347

- Total Living: 1575 s.f.
- Bonus Room: 276 s.f.
- 3 Bedrooms, 2 Baths
- Width: 70'8"
- Depth: 47'4"
- Crawlspace Foundation
- Price Category C

1-800-388-7580
www.affordablehomesforeverystageoflife.com

Donald A. Gardner Architects, Inc.

129

REAR ELEVATION

Welcoming everything from special vacations to becoming grandparents, the affordable homes in this section extend living space to make the most out of everyday life. Whether it's outdoor living areas such as porches, decks and patios, or versatile places like bonus rooms, these extended living spaces accommodate relaxation, entertainment and hobbies, among others. A bonus room can even provide an additional bedroom suite if needed.

Passages
journeys along particular paths

Passages
Donald A. Gardner Architects, Inc.

Contemporary
FARMHOUSE

(Left) An arch replaces columns, creating a grand opening from the foyer to the great room.

(Below) The front porch promotes relaxation, encouraging conversation with passersby.

(Right) Gables and a clerestory window join twin dormers for a charming exterior.

The Larson

❝ Although it's for business, this was the first time I've ever been out of the country. My bags were packed and ready to be loaded in the car. My wallet and passport were on the kitchen counter, and everyone was up early to have coffee with me in the breakfast nook. ❞

(Left) With a wood and wrought-iron morning table, the breakfast nook creates a place for casual meals.

(Below) The dining room's arch captures a view of the front door.

(Right) Molding and wainscoting add sophistication to this formal dining room.

Not an inch was wasted creating a spacious interior for this dormered and gabled country cottage that lives much bigger than it looks on the plan. Front bedroom, master bedroom and open great room/kitchen gain vertical space from cathedral ceilings, while the open foyer pulls the dining room and great room together visually.

The Larson

1-800-388-7580

www.afforadablehomesforeverystageoflife.com

storage

GARAGE
21-0 x 21-4

up

PORCH

skylights

MASTER BED RM.
14-8 x 15-4

BRKFST.
10-4 x 8-6

GREAT RM.
17-4 x 19-0

(cathedral ceiling)

master bath

walk-in closet

fireplace

KITCHEN
11-8 x 10-6

UTIL.
8-8 x 11-0

cl

w
d

linen

bath

sto.

cl

DINING
11-4 x 12-8

FOYER
8-8 x 8-0

cl

BED RM.
12-2 x 12-4

BED RM.
10-10 x 12-4

(cathedral ceiling)

PORCH

FIRST FLOOR

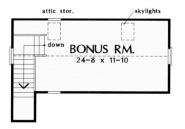

attic stor.

skylights

down

BONUS RM.
24-8 x 11-10

Affordable Homes • The Designs of Donald A. Gardner Architects, Inc.

Passages
Donald A. Gardner Architects, Inc.

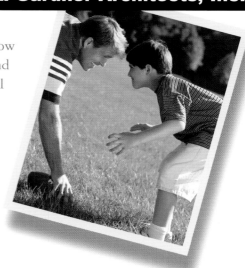

Wraparound front porch, breakfast bay window and skylit back porch add charm and expand living. The master bath pampers with whirlpool tub, separate shower and double lavatories. A bonus room adds flexibility to the plan.

(Far Left) Capturing sun and shade, this wrapping porch gives new meaning to outdoor living.
(Left) With room for two, the master bathroom includes a double vanity.
(Below Left) Modified from the original plan, the garage connects to the house.
(Below) Capping the master bedroom, a soaring cathedral ceiling expands volume.

Plan AHBDG01-360

- Total Living: 1815 s.f.
- Bonus Room: 336 s.f.
- 3 Bedrooms, 2 Baths
- Width: 54'8"
- Depth: 49'6"
- Crawlspace Foundation
- Price Category C

Photographed home may have been modified from the original construction documents.

Passages
Donald A. Gardner Architects, Inc.

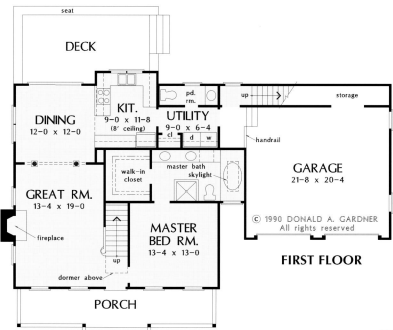

SECOND FLOOR

FIRST FLOOR

© 1990 DONALD A. GARDNER
All rights reserved

The Langford

1-800-388-7580
www.afforadablehomesforeverystageoflife.com

Plan AHBDG01-222

- Total Living: 1557 s.f.
- First Floor: 1057 s.f.
- Second Floor: 500 s.f.
- Bonus Room: 378 s.f.
- 3 Bedrooms, 2-1/2 Baths
- Width: 59'4"
- Depth: 40'0"
- Crawlspace Foundation
- Price Category C

Photographed home may have been modified
from the original construction documents.

Open-Air
INSPIRATION

(Left) Floor-to-ceiling drapes accent the great room's bowed rear wall of windows.

(Below) The stone fireplace creates a dramatic focal point and correlates with the natural surroundings.

(Right) Over the front door, a circle-head clerestory window welcomes light into the foyer.

The Longleaf

❝When we returned from our honeymoon, he carried me across the threshold, bumping my head, because he was laughing. Concerned but laughing even harder, he carried me to the great room and placed me on the sofa. Then he walked into the kitchen for a glass of water and two aspirins. After he took them, he asked me if I wanted some, too.❞

The Longleaf

1-800-388-7580
www.afforadablehomesforeverystageoflife.com

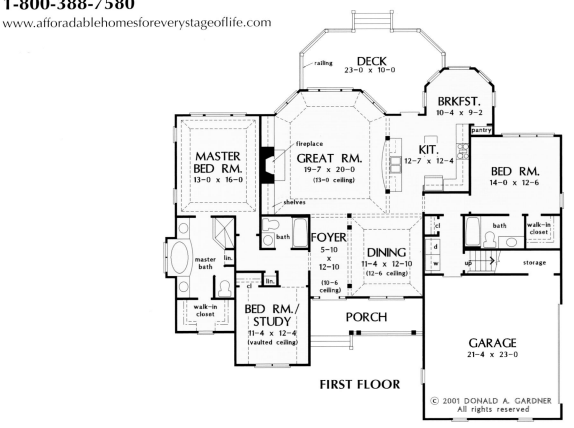

railing

DECK
23-0 x 10-0

BRKFST.
10-4 x 9-2

pantry

fireplace

KIT.
12-7 x 12-4

MASTER BED RM.
13-0 x 16-0

GREAT RM.
19-7 x 20-0
(13-0 ceiling)

BED RM.
14-0 x 12-6

shelves

bath

cl

bath

walk-in closet

master bath

lin.

FOYER
5-10
x
12-10
(10-6 ceiling)

DINING
11-4 x 12-10
(12-6 ceiling)

d

up

storage

walk-in closet

lin.

cl

w

BED RM./ STUDY
11-4 x 12-4
(vaulted ceiling)

PORCH

GARAGE
21-4 x 23-0

FIRST FLOOR

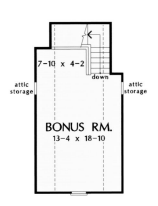

7-10 x 4-2

attic storage

down

attic storage

BONUS RM.
13-4 x 18-10

Affordable Homes • The Designs of Donald A. Gardner Architects, Inc.

This Craftsman cottage combines stone, siding and cedar shake to create striking curb appeal. The interior features an open floorplan with high ceilings, columns and bay windows to visually expand space. On the opposite side of the home an additional bedroom could be used as a second master suite, and above the garage, a bonus room provides ample storage and room to grow.

(Far Left) Wood brackets and cedar shake combine with siding to form a cottage exterior.

(Left) Entertaining continues outside with an open-air living room on the deck.

(Below Left) Turret-styled bays add a touch of Old World character to the rear façade.

(Below) A pass-thru and central island make the kitchen convenient for preparation and serving.

Plan AHBDG01-802

- Total Living: 1971 s.f.
- Bonus Room: 358 s.f.
- 3 Bedrooms, 3 Baths
- Width: 62'6"
- Depth: 57'2"
- Crawlspace Foundation
- Price Category C

Passages
Donald A. Gardner Architects, Inc.

Modern
Mountain Retreat

(Left) A private spot on the rear porch lies just off the secondary bedroom suite.

(Right) A large picture window welcomes natural light into the breakfast nook and kitchen.

(Below) Accented by changing arrangements, tile highlights the counter, creating a backsplash.

The Heathridge

" We spent hours looking all over the house for his first pulled tooth. I had placed it in a jar after we pulled it, but he had taken it out and put it in his pocket. I finally found it stuck in the corner of his pocket when I emptied them to wash his jeans. "

The Heathridge

1-800-388-7580

www.afforadablehomesforeverystageoflife.com

DECK

BRKFST.
13-4 x 10-2

BED RM.
15-0 x 14-8

KITCHEN
13-4 x 11-4

cl

pan.

bath

lin.

pd. rm.

w   d

UTILITY
10-0 x 8-0

cl

GREAT RM.
19-0 x 19-4

(cathedral ceiling)

railing   down

FOYER
7-8 x
9-2   cl

DINING
13-4 x 12-0

PORCH

MASTER BED RM.
15-0 x 17-0

fireplace

walk-in closet   walk-in closet

lin.   master bath

GARAGE
21-0 x 23-2

storage

FIRST FLOOR

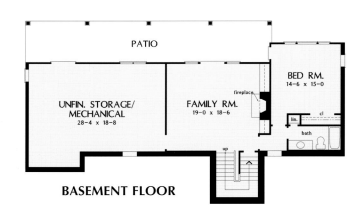

PATIO

UNFIN. STORAGE/ MECHANICAL
28-4 x 18-8

FAMILY RM.
19-0 x 18-6

fireplace

BED RM.
14-6 x 15-0

lin.   cl

bath

up

BASEMENT FLOOR

Affordable Homes • The Designs of Donald A. Gardner Architects, Inc.

This home takes advantage of hillside views with its deck, patio and abundance of rear windows. An open floor plan enhances spaciousness. The great room features a cathedral ceiling, fireplace with built-ins and access to the generous rear deck. Designed for ultimate efficiency, the kitchen effortlessly serves the great room, dining room and breakfast area.

(Far Left) This Craftsman hillside walkout features siding, cedar shake and a barrel-vault entrance.

(Left) The pass-thru is framed in molding and connects the kitchen to the great room.

(Below) A clerestory, transoms and French doors capture the mountain views and natural light.

Plan AHBDG01-763-D

- Total Living: 2998 s.f.
- First Floor: 2068 s.f.
- Basement Floor: 930 s.f.
- 3 Bedrooms, 3-1/2 Baths
- Width: 72'4"
- Depth: 66'0"
- Hillside Walkout Foundation
- Price Category E

Photographed home may have been modified from the original construction documents.

I can't wait to begin our backpacking adventure across Ireland. I'm going to take a lot of photos, and if they turn out, I want one painted as a mural in the dining room.

© 2001 Donald A. Gardner, Inc.

The Englebreit

Plan AHBDG01-929

- Total Living: 1974 s.f.
- 3 Bedrooms, 2 Baths
- Width: 56'0"
- Depth: 58'4"
- Crawlspace Foundation
- Price Category C

1-800-388-7580
www.affordablehomesforeverystageoflife.com

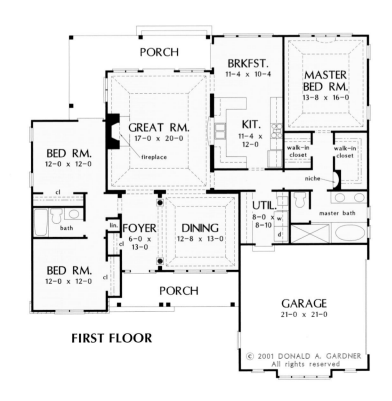

FIRST FLOOR

This is my first house, and mother drove a long way to hold a house-warming for me. She brought some of my friends with her. Having everyone there made my house feel homier.

The Blakely

FIRST FLOOR

REAR ELEVATION

Plan AHBDG01-839

- Total Living: 1399 s.f.
- Bonus Room: 296 s.f.
- 3 Bedrooms, 2 Baths
- Width: 58'0"
- Depth: 44'4"
- Crawlspace Foundation
- Price Category B

1-800-388-7580
www.affordablehomesforeverystageoflife.com

Donald A. Gardner Architects, Inc.

It was her first kiss. Her father wanted to stand in front of the sidelights to detour her boyfriend, but I didn't let him. Instead, he got our son to flicker the porch lights.

The Tanglewood

Plan AHBDG01-757

- Total Living: 1473 s.f.
- Bonus Room: 297 s.f.
- 3 Bedrooms, 2 Baths
- Width: 53'4"
- Depth: 49'8"
- Crawlspace Foundation
- Price Category B

1-800-388-7580
www.affordablehomesforeverystageoflife.com

FIRST FLOOR

DECK

MASTER BED RM. 15-0 x 13-4 (cathedral ceiling)

KITCHEN 10-0 x 13-4

(cathedral ceiling)

GREAT RM. 16-0 x 17-0

fireplace

pan.

walk-in closet

cl

up

master bath

sto.

DINING 10-0 x 12-8

FOYER 7-4 x 7-4

BED RM. 11-0 x 11-0

bath

cl

lin.

cl

BED RM. 11-0 x 11-0

GARAGE 21-0 x 20-0

PORCH

storage

attic storage

BONUS RM. 12-0 x 20-0

down

attic storage

REAR ELEVATION

hey were up early Saturday morning and headed outside after a quick breakfast. The training wheels were off, and after a couple of Band-Aids, she was riding by lunch.

© 2002 Donald A. Gardner, Inc.

The Pemberton

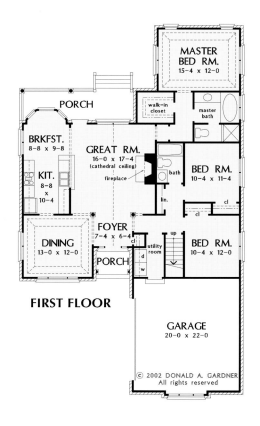

FIRST FLOOR

© 2002 DONALD A. GARDNER
All rights reserved

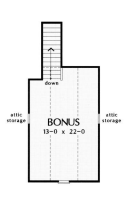

Plan AHBDG01-972

- Total Living: 1608 s.f.
- Bonus Room: 328 s.f.
- 3 Bedrooms, 2 Baths
- Width: 42'7"
- Depth: 72'11"
- Crawlspace Foundation
- Price Category C

1-800-388-7580
www.affordablehomesforeverystageoflife.com

Donald A. Gardner Architects, Inc.

M y son went over to Mom and Dad's to set up their computer in the great room and show them how it operates. Now when I call to see how they're doing, they're usually surfing the net.

© 1999 Donald A. Gardner, Inc.

The Treyburn

Plan AHBDG01-803

- Total Living: 1469 s.f.
- Bonus Room: 383 s.f.
- 3 Bedrooms, 2 Baths
- Width: 63'4"
- Depth: 57'0"
- Crawlspace Foundation
- Price Category B

1-800-388-7580
www.affordablehomesforeverystageoflife.com

REAR ELEVATION   © 1999 Donald A. Gardner, Inc.

I'm glad our floorplan is open, because our baby crawls fast. I can be in any of the common rooms and keep my eyes on her. She'll soon be walking.

© 1999 Donald A. Gardner, Inc.

The Pikeview

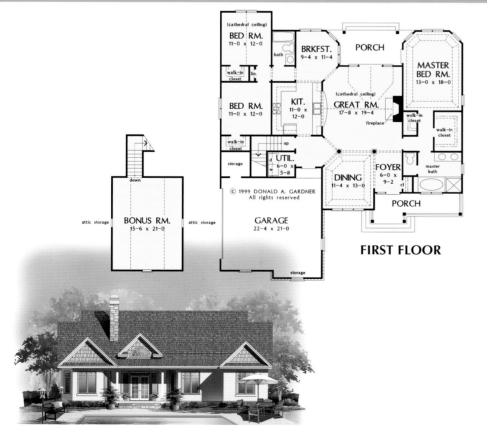

FIRST FLOOR

REAR ELEVATION   © 1999 Donald A. Gardner, Inc.

Plan AHBDG01-805

- Total Living: 1821 s.f.
- Bonus Room: 409 s.f.
- 3 Bedrooms, 2 Baths
- Width: 54'4"
- Depth: 61'6"
- Crawlspace Foundation
- Price Category C

1-800-388-7580
www.affordablehomesforeverystageoflife.com

Donald A. Gardner Architects, Inc.

153

The phone woke us around 2:00 a.m. Our son called us from the hospital. Our daughter-in-law was in labor. By 8 o'clock in the morning, we were grandparents for the first time.

The Westover

Plan AHBDG01-899

- Total Living: 1966 s.f.
- 3 Bedrooms, 2 Baths
- Width: 54'11"
- Depth: 65'9"
- Crawlspace Foundation
- Price Category C

1-800-388-7580
www.affordablehomesforeverystageoflife.com

FIRST FLOOR

We are bracing ourselves for our daughter's first sleepover. The kitchen is stocked with snacks; we rented several movies; and the bonus room is filled with games.

The Templeton

BONUS RM.
13-8 x 21-0

attic storage   down   attic storage

walk-in closet

MASTER BED RM.
15-0 x 13-0

DINING
12-0 x 13-0

PORCH

master bath

bath

BED RM.
11-8 x 12-4

KIT.
11-2 x 11-6

GREAT RM.
15-6 x 15-2

fireplace

w   d
util.

lin.

shelves

walk-in closet

up

cl

FOYER
7-2 X 4-10

cl

BED RM./ STUDY
11-2 x 12-0

PORCH

GARAGE
21-0 x 21-0

FIRST FLOOR

Plan AHBDG01-949

- Total Living: 1610 s.f.
- Bonus Room: 353 s.f.
- 3 Bedrooms, 2 Baths
- Width: 49'11"
- Depth: 55'1"
- Crawlspace Foundation
- Price Category C

1-800-388-7580
www.affordablehomesforeverystageoflife.com

Donald A. Gardner Architects, Inc.

155

REAR ELEVATION

After dinner we sat back down at the table and discussed the importance of credit with her. We are going to allow her to have a credit card under our account and see how it goes.

The Fenmore

Plan AHBDG01-896

- Total Living: 1593 s.f.
- Bonus Room: 332 s.f.
- 3 Bedrooms, 2 Baths
- Width: 50'0"
- Depth: 54'0"
- Crawlspace Foundation
- Price Category C

1-800-388-7580
www.affordablehomesforeverystageoflife.com

FIRST FLOOR

DECK

GREAT RM.
17-8 x 15-8
(vaulted ceiling)
fireplace

BRKFST.
10-0 x 9-8

MASTER BED RM.
14-8 x 13-0

walk-in closet

master bath

KIT.
10-0 x 11-8

UTIL.
6-0 x 9-0

storage

seat

BED RM./STUDY
11-4 x 10-0

FOYER
6-0 x 7-4

DINING
10-0 x 12-0

GARAGE
21-0 x 22-0

bath

cl

lin.

BED RM.
11-4 x 10-0
(vaulted ceiling)

PORCH

BONUS RM.
12-8 x 22-0

attic storage

attic storage

down

Affordable Homes

REAR ELEVATION

I don't know if it was a coincidence or not, but we were sitting on the front porch, and when he drove up, she said "Da Da." Those were her first words.

The Ryley

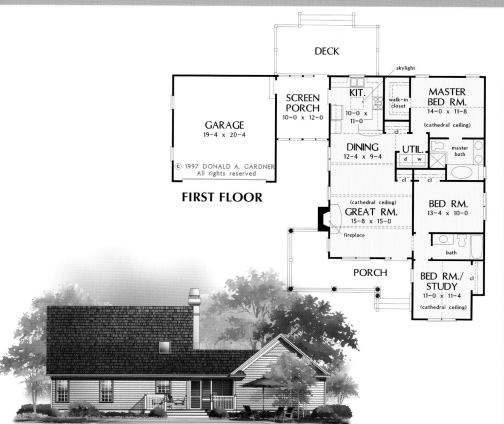

FIRST FLOOR

DECK

SCREEN PORCH
10-0 x 12-0

GARAGE
19-4 x 20-4

skylight

KIT.
10-0 x 11-0

walk-in closet

MASTER BED RM.
14-0 x 11-8
(cathedral ceiling)

DINING
12-4 x 9-4

UTIL.
d w

master bath

GREAT RM.
15-8 x 15-0
(cathedral ceiling)

fireplace

BED RM.
13-4 x 10-0

bath

PORCH

BED RM./ STUDY
11-0 x 11-4
(cathedral ceiling)

REAR ELEVATION

Plan AHBDG01-503

- Total Living: 1246 s.f.
- 3 Bedrooms, 2 Baths
- Width: 60'0"
- Depth: 48'0"
- Crawlspace Foundation
- Price Category B

1-800-388-7580
www.affordablehomesforeverystageoflife.com

Donald A. Gardner Architects, Inc.

157

We loaded up the car, did one final walk-through to make sure everything was off and locked all the doors to the house. This was our first family vacation.

The Nicholson

Plan AHBDG01-1021

- Total Living: 1486 s.f.
- Bonus Room: 341 s.f.
- 3 Bedrooms, 2 Baths
- Width: 52'3"
- Depth: 46'10"
- Crawlspace Foundation
- Price Category B

1-800-388-7580
www.affordablehomesforeverystageoflife.com

FIRST FLOOR

Affordable Homes

REAR ELEVATION   © 2003 Donald A. Gardner, Inc.

I'm glad I made them stop in the utility room, or else my son would have dragged his fish all over the house until he found me. It's the first one he's ever caught.

The Violet

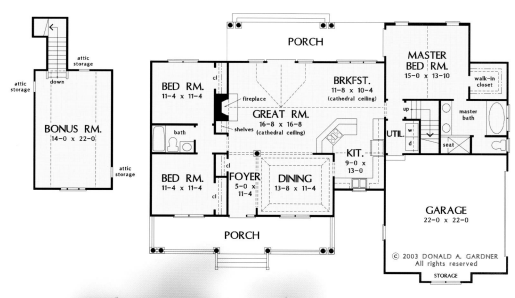

BONUS RM.
14-0 x 22-0

attic storage

attic storage

down

attic storage

PORCH

BED RM.
11-4 x 11-4

fireplace

bath

shelves

GREAT RM.
16-8 x 16-8
(cathedral ceiling)

BRKFST.
11-8 x 10-4
(cathedral ceiling)

MASTER BED RM.
15-0 x 13-10

walk-in closet

up

master bath

UTIL.

w d

seat

BED RM.
11-4 x 11-4

cl

FOYER
5-0 x 11-4

cl

DINING
13-8 x 11-4

KIT.
9-0 x 13-0

GARAGE
22-0 x 22-0

PORCH

STORAGE

FIRST FLOOR

Plan AHBDG01-1016

- Total Living: 1660 s.f.
- Bonus Room: 374 s.f.
- 3 Bedrooms, 2 Baths
- Width: 65'4"
- Depth: 48'8"
- Crawlspace Foundation
- Price Category C

1-800-388-7580
www.affordablehomesforeverystageoflife.com

Donald A. Gardner Architects, Inc.

159

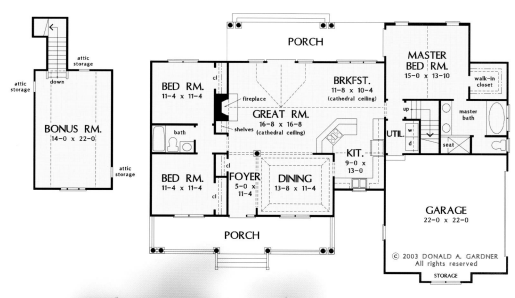

REAR ELEVATION

I discovered the radio show that features local talent after I heard the front door slam and my daughter run into the kitchen squealing for me to turn it on. They played her song.

The Overbrook

Plan AHBDG01-539

- Total Living: 1911 s.f.
- Bonus Room: 406 s.f.
- 3 Bedrooms, 2 Baths
- Width: 62'10"
- Depth: 65'10"
- Crawlspace Foundation
- Price Category C

1-800-388-7580
www.affordablehomesforeverystageoflife.com

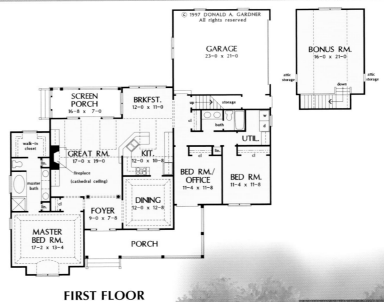

FIRST FLOOR

REAR ELEVATION   © 1997 Donald A. Gardner Architects, Inc.

My husband came home with a handful of brochures, which he taped on our bathroom mirror. I have wanted to visit Alaska my whole life, and we are finally going!

© 1999 Donald A. Gardner, Inc.

The Gibson

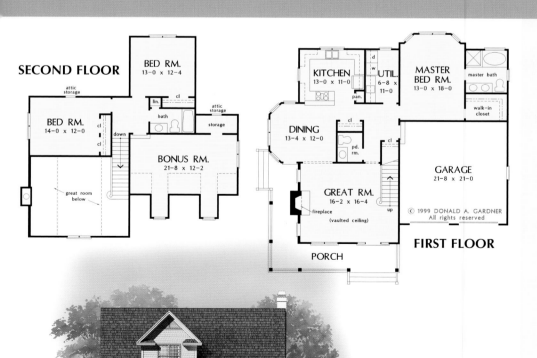

REAR ELEVATION   © 1999 Donald A. Gardner, Inc.

SECOND FLOOR

BED RM.
13-0 x 12-4

attic storage

BED RM.
14-0 x 12-0

BONUS RM.
21-8 x 12-2

great room below

FIRST FLOOR

KITCHEN
13-0 x 11-0

UTIL.
6-8 x 11-0

MASTER BED RM.
13-0 x 18-0

master bath

walk-in closet

DINING
13-4 x 12-0

GREAT RM.
16-2 x 16-4
fireplace
(vaulted ceiling)

GARAGE
21-8 x 21-0

© 1999 DONALD A. GARDNER
All rights reserved

PORCH

Plan AHBDG01-821

- Total Living: 1821 s.f.
- First Floor: 1293 s.f.
- Second Floor: 528 s.f.
- Bonus Room: 355 s.f.
- 3 Bedrooms, 2-1/2 Baths
- Width: 48'8"
- Depth: 50'0"
- Crawlspace Foundation
- Price Category C

1-800-388-7580
www.affordablehomesforeverystageoflife.com

Donald A. Gardner Architects, Inc.

161

My mother had never traveled on a plane before. She drove up to spend the night with us. We stayed up late, talking by the fireplace and then flew out together the next day.

The Jackson

Plan AHBDG01-413

- Total Living: 1417 s.f.
- 3 Bedrooms, 2 Baths
- Width: 69'0"
- Depth: 39'0"
- Crawlspace Foundation
- Price Category B

1-800-388-7580
www.**affordablehomesforeverystage**of**life**.com

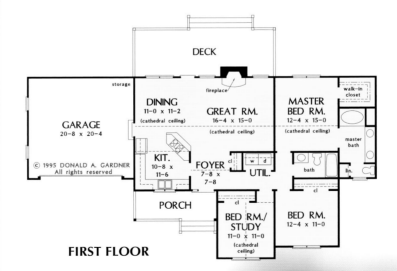

FIRST FLOOR

REAR ELEVATION   © 1995 Donald A. Gardner Architects, Inc.

My son saved his money for an old Mustang he and his father spent months working on. His room and the garage were filled with so many parts that our home looked like an auto store.

© 1994 Donald A. Gardner Architects, Inc.

The Culver

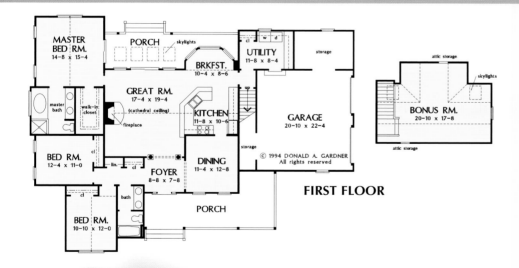

FIRST FLOOR

REAR ELEVATION © 1994 Donald A. Gardner Architects, Inc.

Plan AHBDG01-359

- Total Living: 1807 s.f.
- Bonus Room: 418 s.f.
- 3 Bedrooms, 2 Baths
- Width: 70'8"
- Depth: 53'0"
- Crawlspace Foundation
- Price Category C

1-800-388-7580
www.affordablehomesforeverystageoflife.com

Donald A. Gardner Architects, Inc.

I am an aunt for the first time, and tonight my brother and sister-in-law brought my newborn niece by the house. I have a bassinet in my study for when I babysit.

The Huntington

Plan AHBDG01-714

- Total Living: 1428 s.f.
- Bonus Room: 313 s.f.
- 3 Bedrooms, 2 Baths
- Width: 52'8"
- Depth: 52'4"
- Crawlspace Foundation
- Price Category B

1-800-388-7580
www.affordablehomesforeverystageoflife.com

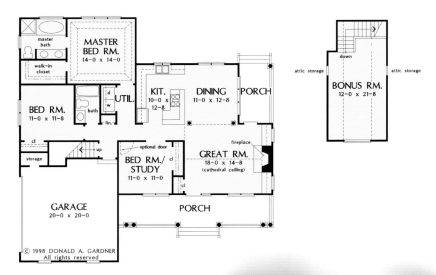

FIRST FLOOR

REAR ELEVATION   © 1998 Donald A. Gardner, Inc.

She uses the study as much as we do. She received a call today, informing her of her scholarship. She switched to speakerphone and asked the man to say it again.

The Sullivan

FIRST FLOOR

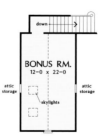

REAR ELEVATION

Plan AHBDG01-513

- Total Living: 1695 s.f.
- Bonus Room: 287 s.f.
- 3 Bedrooms, 2 Baths
- Width: 54'8"
- Depth: 54'4"
- Crawlspace Foundation
- Price Category C

1-800-388-7580
www.affordablehomesforeverystageoflife.com

Donald A. Gardner Architects, Inc.

W e finally built our dream cabin and had the chance to decorate it like we've always wanted to — very rustic and woodsy, which is nothing like our primary home.

The Seymour

Plan AHBDG01-287

- Total Living: 1622 s.f.
- First Floor: 1039 s.f.
- Second Floor: 583 s.f.
- 3 Bedrooms, 2 Baths
- Width: 37'9"
- Depth: 44'8"
- Crawlspace Foundation
- Price Category C

1-800-388-7580
www.affordablehomesforeverystageoflife.com

FIRST FLOOR

PORCH
34-6 x 8-0

walk-in closet

KIT./
DINING
10-10 x 17-8

MASTER
BED RM.
12-0 x 17-0

w   d

bedroom above

sto.

GREAT RM.
17-4 x 17-2

fireplace

master bath

up   cl

PORCH
34-6 x 8-0

SECOND FLOOR

walk-in closet

BED RM.
12-6 x 13-8

bath

closet

down

railing

great room below

BED RM.
12-0 x 15-8

REAR ELEVATION   © 1992 Donald A. Gardner Architects, Inc.

The kids were so excited about their first concert that they went to their rooms and did their homework right away. After dinner, my husband took them to the performance.

© 1999 Donald A. Gardner, Inc.

The Cartwright

Plan AHBDG01-801

- Total Living: 1882 s.f.
- Bonus Room: 363 s.f.
- 3 Bedrooms, 2-1/2 Baths
- Width: 61'4"
- Depth: 55'0"
- Crawlspace Foundation
- Price Category C

1-800-388-7580
www.affordablehomesforeverystageoflife.com

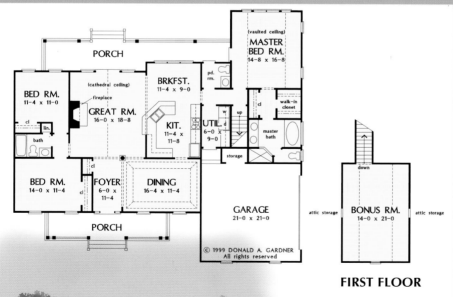

FIRST FLOOR

PORCH

BED RM.
11-4 x 11-0

(cathedral ceiling)
fireplace

GREAT RM.
16-0 x 18-8

BRKFST.
11-4 x 9-0

KIT.
11-4 x
11-8

UTIL.
6-0 x
9-0

(vaulted ceiling)
MASTER
BED RM.
14-8 x 16-8

pd. rm.

walk-in closet

master bath

BED RM.
14-0 x 11-4

FOYER
6-0 x
11-4

DINING
16-4 x 11-4

GARAGE
21-0 x 21-0

storage

PORCH

down

BONUS RM.
14-0 x 21-0

attic storage

attic storage

REAR ELEVATION   © 1999 Donald A. Gardner, Inc.

Donald A. Gardner Architects, Inc.

Prints – What's in a Set?

Each set of Donald A. Gardner plans is a collection of drawings (including components such as floor plans, dimensions, cross sections and elevations) that show you exactly how your house is to be built. Most of our plan packages include:

COVER SHEET

An artist's rendering of the exterior of the house shows you approximately how the house will look when built and landscaped.

FOUNDATION PLAN

This sheet gives the foundation layout, including support walls, excavated and unexcavated areas, if any, and foundation notes. If the foundation is basement rather than monolithic, the plan shows footing and details.

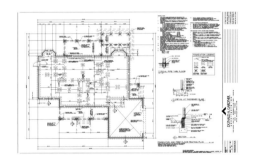

DETAILED FLOOR PLANS

These plans show the layout of each floor of the house. Rooms and interior spaces are carefully dimensioned and keys are given for cross-section details provided later in the plans, as well as window and door size callouts. These plans also show the location of kitchen appliances and bathroom fixtures, as well as suggested locations for electrical fixtures, switches and outlets.

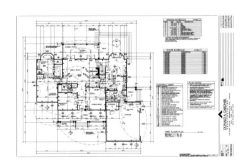

Affordable Homes • The Designs of Donald A. Gardner Architects, Inc.

INTERIOR ELEVATIONS/ROOF PLAN

These drawings show the specific details and design of cabinets, utility rooms, fireplaces, bookcases, built-in units and other special interior features depending on the nature and complexity of the item. The roof plan shows the overall layout and necessary details for roof construction. If trusses are used, we suggest using a local truss manufacturer to design your trusses to comply with local codes and regulations.

EXTERIOR ELEVATIONS/WALL SECTIONS

Included are front, rear, left and right sides of the house. Exterior materials, details and measurements are also given. This sheet also shows details of the house from the roof to the foundation. This section specifies the home's construction, insulation, flooring and roofing details.

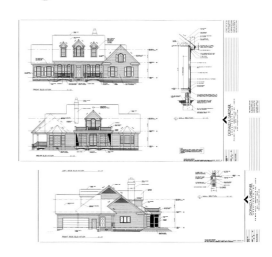

CROSS-SECTION DETAILS

Important changes in floor, ceiling and roof heights or the relationship of one level to another are called out. Also shown, when applicable, are exterior details such as railing and banding.

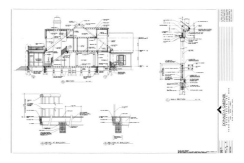

STRUCTURAL PLAN

This sheet gives the overall layout and necessary details for the ceiling, second-floor framing (if applicable) and roof construction.

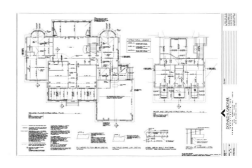

Before You Order

QUICK TURNAROUND

Because you are placing your order directly, we can ship plans to you quickly. If your order is placed Monday through Friday before 11 a.m. EST, we can usually have your plans to you the next business day. Some restrictions may apply. **We cannot ship to a post office box**; please provide a physical street address.

OUR EXCHANGE POLICY

Since our blueprints are printed especially for you at the time you place your order, we cannot accept any returns. If, for some reason, you find that the plan that you purchased does not meet your needs, then you may exchange that plan for another plan in our collection, but all exchanges must be pre-approved by the Customer Service department. We allow you 60 days from the time of purchase to make an exchange. All sets must be returned prior to the exchange taking place. At the time of the exchange, you will be charged a processing fee of 20 percent of the total amount of the original order plus the difference in price between the plans (if applicable) and the cost to ship the new plans to you. Vellums cannot be exchanged. All sets must be approved and authorization given before the exchange can take place. Please call our Customer Service department if you have any questions.

LOCAL BUILDING CODES AND ZONING REQUIREMENTS

Our plans are designed to meet or exceed national building standards. Because of the great differences in geography and climate, each state, county and municipality has its own building codes and zoning requirements. Your plan may need to be modified to comply with local requirements regarding snow loads, energy codes, soil and seismic conditions and a wide range of other matters. Prior to using plans ordered from us, we strongly advise that you consult a local building official.

ARCHITECTURE AND ENGINEERING SEALS

Some cities and states are now requiring that a licensed architect or engineer review and approve any set of building documents prior to construction. This is due to concerns over energy costs, safety, structural integrity and other factors. Prior to applying for a building permit or the start of actual construction, we strongly advise that you consult your local building official who can tell you if such a review is required.

DISCLAIMER

We have put substantial care and effort into the creation of our plans. We authorize the use of our plans on the express condition that you strictly comply with all local building codes, zoning requirements and other applicable laws, regulations and ordinances. However, because we cannot provide on-site consultation, supervision or control over actual construction, and because of the great variance in local building requirements, building practices and soil, seismic, weather and other conditions, WE CANNOT MAKE ANY WARRANTY, EXPRESS OR IMPLIED, WITH RESPECT TO THE CONTENT OR USE OF OUR PRINTS OR VELLUMS, INCLUDING BUT NOT LIMITED TO ANY WARRANTY OF MERCHANTABILITY OR OF FITNESS FOR A PARTICULAR PURPOSE. Please Note: Floor plans are not construction documents and are subject to change. Renderings are artists' concept only.

HOW MANY PRINTS WILL YOU NEED?

We offer a single set of prints so that you can study and plan your dream home in detail. However, you cannot build from this package. One set of blueprints is marked "NOT FOR CONSTRUCTION." If you are planning to get estimates from a contractor or subcontractor, or if you are planning to build immediately, you will need more sets. A single set or "study set" can be upgraded to a larger set package for a nominal fee.

Set packages are less expensive. Make sure you order enough to satisfy all your requirements. Sometimes changes are needed to a plan; in that case we offer vellums that are erasable and reproducible so changes can be made directly to the plans. Vellums are the only set that can be reproduced; it is illegal to copy prints. The following checklist will help determine how many sets you will need:

PLAN CHECKLIST

_____ **Owner (one set for notes, one for file)**

_____ **Builder (generally requires at least three sets; one as a legal document, one for inspections and at least one to give subcontractors)**

_____ **Local Building Department (often requires two sets)**

_____ **Mortgage Lender (usually one set for a conventional loan; three sets for FHA or VA loans)**

_____ **Total Number of Sets**

IGNORING COPYRIGHT LAWS CAN BE A
$1,000,000 Mistake!

Recent changes in the US copyright laws allow for statutory penalties of up to $150,000 per incident for copyright infringement involving any of the copyrighted plans found in this publication. The law can be confusing. So, for your own protection, take the time to understand what you cannot do when it comes to home plans.

What You Can't Do!

- **You Cannot Duplicate Home Plans.**
- **You Cannot Copy Any Part Of A Home Plan To Create Another.**
- **You Cannot Build A Home Without Buying A Blueprint Or License.**
- **You Cannot Build A Home From A Study Set. Study Sets Do Not Include Licenses.**

How To Order

Donald A. Gardner Architects, Inc.
150 Executive Center Drive, Ste. 215
Greenville, SC 29615

1-800-388-7580
www.affordablehomesforeverystageoflife.com

Additional Items
Blueprints (per set)..$ 60.00
Full Reverse Blueprints.................................$125.00

Materials List
Plan Categories A - E ....$ 65.00
Plan Category F - L..$ 75.00

Basement Plans
Plan Categories A - C....................................$225.00
Plan Categories D - E....................................$250.00
Plan Category F - L..$275.00

11" x 17" Color Front Perspective Rendering* $100.00
Specification Outline*....................................$ 15.00
*Call for availability

Shipping & Handling
Overnight ....$ 40.00
Priority Overnight ....$ 50.00
2nd Day...$ 32.00
Ground ....$ 20.00
Saturday (If available) ....$ 50.00
International Delivery (Please call for prices & availability).

PLAN PRICE SCHEDULE

	1 Study Set	4 Sets	8 Sets	Vellum
A	$455	$505	$555	$710
B	$500	$550	$600	$775
C	$545	$595	$645	$840
D	$590	$640	$690	$905
E	$635	$685	$735	$970
F	$680	$730	$780	$1035
G	$755	$805	$855	$1115
H	$830	$880	$930	$1195
I	$930	$980	$1030	$1295
J	$1030	$1080	$1130	$1395
K	$1130	$1180	$1230	$1495
L	$1230	$1280	$1330	$1595

➤ *Prices subject to change without notice.*

Order Form

Plan Number _____

- ☐ 1-set (study only) ....$_____
- ☐ 4-set building package ....$_____
- ☐ 8-set building package ....$_____
- ☐ 1-set of reproducible vellums ....$_____

___ Additional Identical Plans @ $60 each $_____

___ Full Reverse Plans @ $125 each $_____

___ Basement Plans (See pricing above) $_____

Sub-Total $_____

Shipping and Handling $_____

Sales Tax (SC Res.) 5% $_____

Total $_____

Check one: ☐Visa ☐MasterCard ☐AmEx ☐Discover

Credit Card Number _____

Expiration Date _____

Signature _____

Name_____

Company_____

Street _____

City _____ State____ Zip _____

Daytime Telephone Number (_____) _____

Check one:
☐Consumer ☐Builder ☐Developer

Index

Top Ten Affordability Questions You Should Ask Before Building a Home

• **What is your budget?**

Choose a home that costs no more than four times your current salary (excluding bonuses and potential raises).

• **What will be included in your mortgage financing?**

Think about insurance, property taxes and escrow figures, and how these will be factored into your monthly mortgage payment.

• **Have you picked an affordable location?**

Building in a relatively flat suburb, for example, will be cheaper than building in a coastal or mountain location.

• **What type of lot will you build on?**

Every lot varies in dimension, surface and elevation. Choose a home that is best suited for the lot you have acquired.

• **What type of extra fees will you have to include in your budget?**

Building permits, property owner's association dues and other often-unconsidered fees can add up quickly. Make sure you're aware of these and include them in your home-building budget.

• **Are there any regulations to your land usage?**

Become familiar with local zoning laws and any covenants you may be required to meet. Both factors can contribute to the affordability of your home.

• **What are your home's specifications?**

The more square footage in a home, typically, the more expensive it will be to build. Choose a square footage that accommodates all of your family's needs...and your budget!

• **What materials will you use to build your home?**

With a wide array of product choices, choose those that are long-lasting and low maintenance, which may not save money up front, but will in the long run.

• **How will labor costs impact your total building budget?**

The more materials you use that requires specialists, the higher the cost.

• **What will your utilities cost?**

Consider what it will cost to prep your land for construction and occupancy with regards to water and power needs.